EATS

EATS

enjoy all the seconds

135 COLOURFUL RECIPES TO SAVOUR & SAVE

MARY ROLPH LAMONTAGNE

Published by Advantage, Charleston, South Carolina.
Member of Advantage Media Group.

ADVANTAGE is a registered trademark and the Advantage colophon is a trademark of Advantage Media Group, Inc.

ISBN: 978-1-59932-386-2
LCCN: 2013932687

This publication is designed to provide accurate and authoritative information in regard to the subject matter covered. It is sold with the understanding that the publisher is not engaged in rendering legal, accounting, or other professional services. If legal advice or other expert assistance is required, the services of a competent professional person should be sought. Printed in China.

Advantage Media Group is proud to be a part of the Tree Neutral® program. Tree Neutral offsets the number of trees consumed in the production and printing of this book by taking proactive steps such as planting trees in direct proportion to the number of trees used to print books. To learn more about Tree Neutral, please visit **www.treeneutral.com**. To learn more about Advantage's commitment to being a responsible steward of the environment, please visit **www.advantagefamily.com/green**

Advantage Media Group is a publisher of business, self-improvement, and professional development books and online learning. We help entrepreneurs, business leaders, and professionals share their Stories, Passion, and Knowledge to help others Learn & Grow. Do you have a manuscript or book idea that you would like us to consider for publishing? Please visit **advantagefamily.com** or call **1.866.775.1696**.

"There is no love sincerer than the love of food."
—GEORGE BERNARD SHAW

*To my mother, Beverley, a woman who taught
me the importance of living life to the fullest
through food, friends and travel.*

*To Paul, Charlotte, Patrick and Frédéric. Time
and time again, you have followed me on our
many adventures. I could not have asked for a
better family to have by my side through the good,
the bad and everything in between.*

Duba Plains Camp, Botswana

Thank you

I was once told, as I was having my astrological chart done, that I was born to write a book. At last, the time has come!

All of this could not have been a reality if I did not have my wonderful right hand woman by my side. Thank you Ruth for always being open to testing new recipes, sharing your knowledge of local African delicacies and being willing to give honest feedback during our tasting sessions.

Photography has always been an interest of mine but I realized early on that if I was to produce quality pictures to compliment my recipes, I was going to need some guidance. From a young age, on family trips, we always traveled with cameras in hand but photographing food was a foreign concept. Thank you Alice for stepping up and introducing me to the intricacies of food photography. I could not have made it through without you.

The safari/animal pictures in this book are a compilation of pictures collected from family and friends over the past eight years. I want to thank all of you for sharing your photos with me. A special thank you to Frederic for clicking away on our many safari adventures.

In Africa, it is said that it takes a village to raise a child. I would say the same about writing a book. I have called upon so many family and friends around the world to give me their advice, taste my recipes and support me when everything seemed to be going pear shaped. I thank you from the bottom of my heart.

Having a strong team behind the scenes is also very important. Once I decided to take the self-publishing route, I realized the necessity of good editing and design. So thank you to Joy from Bushbaby, Alison and Amy from Advantage Group and Cynthia and Brigitte, my eagle eye proof readers. Your endless support and praise was highly valued.

Finally, thank you to my family and their belief in me…If it was not for my husband Paul, luring us to South Africa, I would not have had the African bush to inspire me to finally write about my passions: food and reducing waste.

Contents

Weavers nest at Babylonstoren, South Africa

Introduction

ALL THE OTHER KIDS ON THE BLOCK were eating "Wonderbread". They were allowed pizza and soda for their birthday parties and, come November, my peers were still sucking on lollipops weeks after the fun of Halloween was behind them.

Celebrating Cynthia's birthday in my highchair

Things were different in my household. I was served wholewheat loaves from the Cuckoo Clock, my mother's go-to natural food store in Montreal, Canada. Our birthday parties were catered with dishes foreign to my peers, such as chicken à la king and vol-au-vent. Halloween candy eating lasted only two days. Following our trick or treating adventures, my siblings and I were allowed to choose a plateful of candy, which became our dinner on November 1st. Anything not consumed that night was discarded and we returned to our regular diets.

Granny and I in her garden

As I look back on my relatively strict childhood, I realize how grateful I am for my upbringing and how much my mother influenced the way I have raised my own children. Fresh food has always been an important aspect of my life and now I get to share that with my own family.

Of course, my mother is not the only person who has influenced my relationship with food over the years. My first memories of kitchen gardens are from my grandparents, who cultivated a small fertile plot during the three-month growing season in Northern Quebec. Visits to our grandparents' lake house were always memorable. I remember racing out of our wood-panelled station wagon to collect my grandmother's aging basket. With her rust-licked clippers and mud-covered eggshell-blue gloves waiting for me, I would rush off into the manicured veggie patch to find what treats nature had to offer.

Thirty-five years later, living on the outskirts of Cape Town with my three children and husband,

Ski holiday at Sugarloaf in Maine

I have finally created my own edible treasures. Mother Nature is not always as cooperative as I would like, but I can now appreciate what farmers must experience on a daily basis. Though we do not have the fears of an early frost such as in Canada, I have learned that the position of the sun, the size and types of plants, the level of mulch and so much more, all play an integral part in the well-being of a productive fruit and vegetable garden.

2005 Family bush experience at Ngala game lodge, Krueger Park, South Africa

If someone had told me eight years ago that I would be growing my own vegetables, cultivating a worm farm and raising chickens, I would have laughed in disbelief. Back then, companion planting, natural predators and worm farms were part of someone else's story. My priority, at the time as a trained chef was finding the best quality produce for the best possible price. Bottom-line profits were always the primary influence on who would be the best supplier. Sadly, quality and local did not always play a prominent part in the decision-making process.

My true food and leftover epiphany occurred while working at game farms (safari lodges) throughout Southern Africa, where fresh food is not readily available and waste is charged for by the bag. I began to look at produce and discarded

food in a new light. While my job was to recreate menus and train kitchen staff, I found myself making seasonal, local and leftover foods my main mission. I began to rethink the way food was being treated. Rather than throwing away an entire bowl of quinoa salad, why not revive it into mini fritters that would be the base for a lemon-scented crème fraîche and smoked salmon trout appetizer?

My move to South Africa in 2005 was meant to be a one, maximum two-year posting. I am grateful for the time I have spent in my newly adopted land and am always so excited to meet individuals who can help me inch forward towards full clarity on the issues of creating memorable food while reducing our foodie footprint. Here, in Cape Town, we are blessed with some brilliant choices of fresh produce. Though not always organic, the fruits and vegetables are grown to not only feed the population but to also support small, independent farmers. The culture of creating one's own kitchen garden is also growing. Families now have their own food and no longer have empty bellies.

We all have to eat. Waste will always be produced. It is time to celebrate the small steps each of us take to create delicious food while also reducing our waste and food footprint.

The challenge to myself and everyone else is to rethink waste and celebrate by creating new dishes from leftovers or recycling certain food items into another use. If we all take baby steps, we might be pleasantly surprised by the outcome.

Celebrating Christmas in Cape Town, South Africa

How to navigate EATS

HEALTH BENEFITS:

Offers nutritional tidbits about each fruit and vegetable

BUYING AND STORING GUIDE:

Offers tips on what to look for when buying fresh fruit and vegetables, as well as helpful advice on how they can be stored to keep them at their best for as long as possible.

GREEN FINGERS:

Proposes a number of options to re-use rather than throw out the rotting items in your fridge. Hints for kitchen gardens are also discussed.

Master recipes

Every vegetable and fruit in this book has a master recipe that can be used for an initial meal. Any of these recipes can then be reinvented for another 3-4 recipes.

Most of the fruit recipes can be used as the master recipe or in its natural, uncooked state, unless otherwise mentioned in the recipe.

Indexes

Two types of indexes are found at the end of the book,

1) listing the recipes by course.

2) listing the recipes by ingredient.

Get on your journey and start to better understand how to utilize food in a more creative and responsible way. I dare you.

Safari pictures

Working in safari camps inspired me to write this book. The animal photographs throughout this book are an ode to these beautiful creatures that need to be respected and protected.

Other things you should know:

- I do not make any distinction between salted and unsalted butter.
  Use whichever you prefer.

- I have used eggs of 60g/2.10oz.

- All milk used is 2% milk, unless stated otherwise.

- All herbs used are fresh, unless stated otherwise.

- For the fruit sections, all fruits can be used raw or prepared as in the master recipes unless stated otherwise.

Certain ingredients are known by different names, depending on where you are on the planet. To make it easier for you, I've included a list of the terms I have used as well as the alternative names by which they are known:

Term used in the book	Also known as
almonds, flaked	almonds, slivered
rocket	arugula
cilantro	coriander, dhania
eggplant	aubergine, brinjal
zucchini	courgette, baby marrow
prawns	shrimp
biltong	jerky
spring onion, green onion	scallion
icing sugar	confectioner's sugar
bicarbonate of soda	baking soda
cornflour	cornstarch
mealie meal	corn meal
heavy cream	whipping cream
vanilla essence	vanilla
flat leaf parsley	Italian parsley
cherry tomato	rosa tomato
castor sugar	superfine sugar
chilli	chili pepper
flour	cake flour
beetroot	beets

THE GREENS

Zebra crossing during the Wildebeest migration, Serengeti, Tanzania

Asparagus

As a child, asparagus was a vegetable that caused endless confusion for me. I could not understand how we were repeatedly told not to use our fingers to eat our food, yet my grandmother would pick up individual spears and slurp them into her mouth without a care. My inquisitive stare was always met with "That is how the queen eats her asparagus". To this day, I have a hard time eating asparagus with my fingers, queen or no queen.

Master recipe

Cooked asparagus

SERVES 2-4

500g (1 lb) fresh asparagus

2 tablespoons oil (olive or grapeseed), not butter because it will burn

sea salt and pepper

Roast

▸ Preheat the oven to 200°C (400°F).

▸ Place the asparagus in a large roasting pan, pour over the oil and toss to coat well.

▸ Season with salt and pepper.

▸ Roast in the oven for 8-10 minutes – the asparagus should still be slightly crunchy.

Sauté

▸ Heat the oil in a cast-iron frying pan.

▸ Place the asparagus in the pan, in a single layer.

▸ Sauté for 4–5 minutes – the asparagus should still be slightly crunchy.

Boil

▸ Bring a saucepan of water to a boil. Add salt.

▸ Add the asparagus and cook in the simmering water for 5–8 minutes – the asparagus should still be slightly crunchy.

▸ Drain and reserve the cooking water to be used as a stock.

▸ Drizzle with your favorite olive oil. Season to taste with salt and pepper.

HEALTH BENEFITS

Asparagus is effective in helping to prevent urinary tract infections and kidney stones.

These little green spears are rich in potassium, vitamin A and folate, which helps in the prevention of many cancers, premature aging and inflammation.

For some, asparagus is believed to be an aphrodisiac… due to its shape and not its chemical compounds!

Because of its high level of vitamin K, asparagus is particularly effective in the prevention of osteoporosis and osteoarthritis.

BUYING AND STORING GUIDE

Select smooth, green, straight stocks that do not have any wrinkles near the cut ends. Check that the tips are tightly closed.

Do not wash asparagus before storing; rather trim the ends and stand the stalks upright in a little water with a plastic bag covering the spears.

Asparagus can be stored in the refrigerator for 2–3 days.

To freeze asparagus, blanch in boiling water for 1–2 minutes and then dunk in ice water to stop the cooking process. Place in a single layer in an airtight container and store in the freezer for up to 3 months.

GREEN FINGERS

Asparagus are spring plants that take three years to mature before they can be harvested. They are royal in my mind since these plants come from crowns.

Asparagus prefer cool temperatures and a good water supply. A winter frost is necessary to allow the plant to lay dormant for a few months.

When the harvest season is over, let the plant grow to strengthen itself for the following year's crop.

Asparagus can be grown in a container but will yield only small quantities, so consider the beautiful fern-like plants an educational rather than a feeding plant.

Lemon-scented asparagus quinoa

SERVES 6–8

Quinoa has become mainstream in the US but this powerful grain is still a novelty in South Africa. The earthy grain flavour creates a lovely contrast to the freshness of the asparagus.

1 cup quinoa

2 cups water

1 tablespoon finely chopped shallot

2 teaspoons lemon zest

2 tablespoons lemon juice

3 tablespoons extra virgin olive oil

1 tablespoon capers, drained

2 tablespoons minced fresh flat-leaf parsley

1 tablespoon minced fresh chives

salt and pepper

1 cup cooked, chopped asparagus (master recipe, see p. 11)

¼ cup Parmesan cheese shavings

¼ cup toasted pine nuts

▶ Rinse the quinoa well under cold water then place in a saucepan with the 2 cups of water. Bring to a boil, then turn down the heat and simmer until the water is absorbed, about 15 minutes.

▶ Prepare a vinaigrette by mixing the shallot, lemon zest and lemon juice together in a small bowl. Whisk in the olive oil, then add capers, parsley and chives. Season to taste with salt and pepper. Set aside.

▶ When the quinoa is cooked, transfer it to a large mixing bowl and incorporate the vinaigrette with a fork or large spoon to combine.

▶ Gently stir in the asparagus and garnish with Parmesan shavings and toasted pine nuts.

Quinoa is a versatile grain. Use leftovers, mixed with egg and seasoning and fry to make mini cakes (see p. 51). Serve topped with a sliver of prosciutto, arugula and crème fraîche. Store pine nuts in the freezer to extend their shelf life.

Asparagus risotto

SERVES 6

This is a great risotto recipe that uses lemon and asparagus as its flavour boosters. Feel free to experiment with other vegetables and cheeses to create your own signature risotto.

3 cups chicken stock (or vegetable stock for a vegetarian option)

2 tablespoons olive oil

¼ cup minced onion

1 cup arborio rice

¼ cup dry white wine

½ teaspoon lemon zest

¼ cup soft goat's cheese

½ cup freshly grated Parmesan cheese

1 cup cooked, chopped asparagus (master recipe, see p. 19)

Salt and pepper

1 teaspoon butter

Pea shoots (optional)

▸ Bring the stock to a simmer in a saucepan.

▸ In a separate medium-sized saucepan, heat 2 tablespoons of oil over medium heat. Add the onion and cook for a few minutes until translucent. Add the rice and cook for 2 minutes more, stirring until nicely coated and opaque in colour. Add the wine and stir until most of it has been absorbed.

▸ Add ½ cup of stock to the rice, stirring continuously until the liquid is almost completely absorbed. Add more stock in ½ cup increments and repeat this process until the rice is tender, but still firm to the bite, 15–20 minutes. Remove from the heat.

▸ Gently stir in the lemon zest, goat's cheese, Parmesan and the asparagus. Add salt and pepper to taste and the butter. Cover and set aside for 3–5 minutes.

▸ Serve with a garnish of Parmesan shavings and pea shoots.

The stock amount given is approximate. You may need a little more or less. If you end up needing more stock and you find yourself without, just use water or any reserved cooking water from boiling vegetables. As long as you have a vegetable, some fresh herbs and cheese, risotto becomes an easy dish to whip up for a quick meal or a great side dish.

Asparagus and wild mushroom bread pudding

SERVES 6 AS A MAIN COURSE OR 8 AS A SIDE DISH

Using the basic ratio of ¾ cup of liquid (cream and milk) to 1 egg will ensure a creamy mixture. Add some herbs and vegetables for savoury, and spices and sugar for sweet bread puddings.

Working in hotels, and especially game reserves, made me realize that there was always a surplus of bread. Bread puddings, especially savoury ones, are a great way to feed a crowd and use up leftovers.

Ingredients	
3 cups milk	
2 cloves garlic, quartered	
4 eggs	
¼ cup chopped fresh flat-leaf parsley	
1 tablespoon chopped fresh thyme	
Salt and pepper	
4 cups cubed stale bread	
1 cup cooked, chopped asparagus (master recipe, see p. 19)	
1 cup mushroom pieces (master recipe, see p. 221)	
1 cup grated Emmenthal cheese	
2 tablespoons grated Parmesan cheese	
1 tablespoon truffle oil	

▶ Warm the milk and garlic and then set aside for 30 minutes.

▶ Beat the eggs together, then add the milk, parsley, thyme, salt and pepper.

▶ In a separate bowl, mix together the bread pieces, asparagus, mushrooms and Emmenthal. Transfer to a well buttered, medium-sized gratin dish.

▶ Pour the milk and egg mixture over the bread mixture.

▶ Sprinkle with Parmesan cheese.

▶ Set aside for as long as possible, or even overnight, pressing down on the mixture on a regular basis to ensure that the bread is well soaked.

▶ Preheat the oven to 180°C (350°F). Bake for 35–40 minutes, or until browned and puffed up and a knife inserted into the centre comes out clean.

▶ This is great as a vegetarian option or a side to have with poached eggs and bacon... at brunch.

Poached egg on an asparagus, potato and pancetta pillow

SERVES 4

Leftover potatoes and asparagus are the perfect stars in this recipe. It works well for brunch, served with a mimosa and a crusty loaf of bread. Leftover spinach (p. 37) can be substituted for the asparagus.

Cooked asparagus can be added to so many dishes, whether it be a salad, potatoes or a frittata. The key is not to overcook it when you first serve it. Be sure it has a crunch to it.

½ cup mashed potatoes (or leftover boiled potatoes)

¼ cup chopped pancetta

¼ cup chopped onion

1 clove garlic, chopped

2 tablespoons flour

1 tablespoon oil, for frying potato cakes

8 asparagus spears (master recipe, see p. 19)

4 eggs

1 teaspoon rice vinegar (or white)

Horseradish sauce

1 tablespoon prepared horseradish cream

½ cup plain or Greek yoghurt

1 teaspoon lemon zest

1 teaspoon lemon juice

Potato and pancetta pillow

▸ Place the mashed potatoes in a small bowl or mash leftover boiled potatoes.

▸ In a small frying pan, cook the pancetta until crispy. Add the onion and garlic and fry until the onions have softened. Add this mixture to the mashed potatoes and combine well.

▸ Divide the potato mixture into four then use your hands to create four round patties (somewhat like a burger patty).

▸ Lightly coat the patties with the flour.

▸ Heat the oil in a medium-sized frying pan and gently add the patties.

▸ Cook on one side until browned, then flip over and cook the other side.

▸ Once cooked, transfer to a baking sheet and place in a warm oven.

Horseradish sauce

▸ Mix the horseradish, yoghurt, lemon juice and zest together in a small bowl. Set aside.

▸ Reheat the asparagus spears.

Poached egg

▸ Bring a medium-sized saucepan half-filled with water and a teaspoon of vinegar to a simmer. Swirl the water with a spoon to create a whirlpool.

▸ Crack one egg at a time into the water whirlpool and cook for 3 minutes for a soft egg.

▸ Remove from the water with a slotted spoon and serve on top of the potato cake with asparagus and horseradish cream.

For the perfect poached egg, I was taught at chef school to create a little vortex in the water as you add the egg and to use very fresh eggs. The vinegar in the water helps to coagulate the whites of the eggs. I prefer rice vinegar because the flavour is not as strong as white vinegar.

Broccoli

My girlfriend, Natalie, was a big fan of broccoli. Sadly, she succumbed to breast cancer in 2010. She was a firm believer that broccoli was a key to her surviving for years beyond what she was given. I love to grow these mini trees in my garden because they are a reminder of her drive to survive.

Master recipe

Broccoli prepared to perfection

SERVES 4 AS A SIDE DISH

Boil

1 large head of broccoli, cut into small florets and stalks thinly sliced

1 tablespoon olive oil

A squeeze of lemon

Sea salt and pepper

▸ Bring a large saucepan of water to a rolling boil. Add salt and then the broccoli.

▸ Cook for 10 minutes – the broccoli should still have a slight crunch.

▸ Strain and reserve cooking water to use as a vegetable stock.

▸ Drizzle with olive oil and lemon juice. Season to taste.

Sauté

1 tablespoon olive oil

1 clove garlic, minced

1 large head of broccoli, cut into small florets and stalks thinly sliced

1 cup vegetable or chicken broth

Sea salt and pepper

▸ Heat oil in medium frying pan.

▸ Add garlic and sauté until softened (2-3 minutes).

▸ Add broccoli and sauté for an additional few minutes.

▸ Pour in stock and continue cooking until broccoli is *al dente*.

HEALTH BENEFITS

High in fibre, broccoli is a fat burner since it takes more calories to eat it than the number of calories in it.

Vitamin B6 and folate in broccoli help to reduce the risk of heart disease.

Broccoli is rich in anti-oxidants, which helps in combatting a number of different cancers.

These mini green trees are immune system boosters, bone strengtheners and skin beautifiers due to their high levels of vitamin C, vitamin K, beta-carotene and potassium.

Eat more florets since that is where all the beta-carotene is stored.

BUYING AND STORING GUIDE

Look for firm green leaves, plump stalks and tight green heads without any yellow flowers. Yellow flowers and woody stalks are signs of broccoli that is past due.

Broccoli needs to be cut into small florets and blanched prior to being frozen.

Broccoli needs to be consumed within 10 days of being picked. It can be refrigerated in a perforated plastic bag or wrapped loosely in damp paper towels.

GREEN FINGERS

This member of the cabbage family can be grown in the garden as well as in a container in your home or on your balcony.

Once considered an exotic vegetable, broccoli grows best in cooler climates.

Feed your worms or compost pile the end bits from the broccoli, though very little needs to be thrown away.

Broccoli, olive and tomato pasta

SERVES 6

Almost anything can be used to make pesto as long as you have a master flavour, good olive oil, nuts and some cheese. In this recipe I use broccoli to make the pesto and any leftovers can be frozen for later use.

Broccoli pesto (makes 1–1¼ cups)

1 cup cooked broccoli (master recipe, see p. 27)

1 clove garlic

¼ cup roasted almonds, chopped

1 tablespoon chopped fresh basil

1 tablespoon lemon juice

½ cup Parmesan cheese

½-¾ cup olive oil

salt and pepper

Olive and tomato pasta

¼ cup Kalamata olives, halved and pitted

½ cup baby tomatoes, halved

½ round buffalo mozzarella, cut into bite-sized pieces

3 cups uncooked bowtie pasta

Sea salt and pepper

2 tablespoons chopped fresh parsley

1 tablespoon chopped fresh basil

For pesto

▸ Combine all the pesto ingredients in a blender until you have achieved a slightly lumpy consistency. Add a little more olive oil if the pesto seems too dry.

For pasta

▸ In a large serving bowl, mix together 1 cup of broccoli pesto, olives, tomatoes and mozzarella pieces.

▸ In a large stock pot, bring salted water to a boil and cook the pasta until *al dente* (slightly firm).

▸ Reserve ½ cup of pasta water and drain the pasta.

▸ Mix the pasta with the pesto, vegetables and cheese. Allow the hot pasta to melt the cheese and create its own sauce. If it's too dry, add a little pasta water.

▸ Season with salt and pepper and sprinkle parsley and basil over the pasta.

▸ Stir and serve.

Broccoli pesto can be saved and refrigerated for 5 days and frozen for a few months.

Pesto is also good on a grilled tomato and cheese sandwich.

Broccoli and chèvre soufflé

SERVES 8

Do not be afraid of making soufflés. The key is in the timing and the way the cook mixes the stiff egg whites into the flavourful base. Gentle hands and as little folding as possible are the key ingredients.

3 tablespoons butter

2 tablespoons flour

1 cup milk

1 cup cooked broccoli (master recipe, see p. 27)

½ cup soft chèvre, crumbled

6 eggs, room temperature, separated

½ teaspoon cayenne pepper

Sea salt

1 tablespoon dried breadcrumbs

▶ Preheat the oven to 180°C (350°F).

▶ Melt 2 tablespoons of butter in a small saucepan, and add the flour. Cook for a few minutes before adding the milk.

▶ When the mixture begins to thicken, add the broccoli and chèvre. Remove from the heat and cool slightly.

▶ Add the egg yolks and season with cayenne pepper and salt.

▶ Pour the mixture into a separate large mixing bowl and allow to cool completely.

▶ In another bowl, beat the egg whites to stiff peaks.

▶ Carefully combine half of the egg whites into the broccoli mixture, then gently fold the remaining egg whites into the mixture.

▶ Prepare 8 individual ramekins by greasing them with the remaining tablespoon of butter and sprinkling breadcrumbs in each ramekin. Pour the mixture into the ramekins, up to the rim.

▶ Bake for 20 minutes until puffed and golden. Serve immediately with a green salad.

Eggs at room temperature will give greater volume to your egg whites. To bring eggs to room temperature, place them in a warm waterbath for 5–10 minutes.

I make my own breadcrumbs from stale baguette that I dry out, pass through a food processor and store in the freezer.

1 large head of broccoli chopped into small pieces = 1 cup cooked broccoli.

The shallot can be replaced with scallion or regular onion.

Cheesy broccoli cocktail bites

MAKES 24

These are very versatile and can be frozen, once cooked, for surprise guests. I sometimes replace the broccoli with spinach and add little pieces of biltong for meat lovers in the safari camps. Prosciutto or bacon also works well.

Ingredients	Method
4 eggs	▸ Preheat the oven to 180°C (350°F). Grease a mini-muffin pan.
1 cup milk	▸ Whisk the eggs, milk, Dijon mustard and flour together in a large bowl.
2 teaspoons Dijon mustard	▸ Heat the olive oil in a skillet and sauté the shallot and garlic. Add the broccoli and sauté for another minute until the pieces break up easily.
⅓ cup flour	
1 tablespoon olive oil	▸ Combine the broccoli and the milk mixture, and then add the Cheddar cheese.
1 shallot, minced	
1 clove garlic, minced	▸ Transfer the broccoli mixture into the prepared muffin pan.
2 cups cooked broccoli (master recipe, see p. 27)	▸ Sprinkle with Parmesan cheese.
1 cup grated extra strong Cheddar cheese	▸ Bake for 20–30 minutes, or until the broccoli bites have a golden brown crust.
¼ cup grated Parmesan cheese	
¼ teaspoon cayenne pepper	

These bites are so versatile. They can also be cooked in larger ramekins for a vegetarian option. If there are any leftovers, they can be easily frozen.

Crusted tilapia served on a spicy broccoli purée

SERVES 4

This is an easy, no-fail fish recipe that my whole family enjoys. The broccoli base adds a nice bit of spice to the fragrant fish. This purée can also be used for other grilled meats.

Chilli seeds are where all the heat is hidden so be sure to remove them if you don't like it too spicy.

Broccoli purée

¾ cup whipping cream

1 thumbnail-sized piece of fresh ginger, peeled

1 clove garlic, halved

2 cups cooked broccoli florets and stems (master recipe, see p. 27)

½ jalapeño chilli pepper, seeded and chopped

Salt and pepper

Crusted tilapia

1 cup dried breadcrumbs

12 fresh mint leaves, chopped

¼ cup chopped fresh coriander

2 tablespoons olive oil

2 cloves garlic

1 tablespoon grated fresh ginger

¼ cup soy sauce

2 tablespoons lemon juice

4 tilapia fillets

For the broccoli purée

▸ Bring cream to a simmer in a small saucepan on the stove, then switch off the heat. Add the piece of ginger and the garlic halves and allow to steep in the cream for 20 minutes, then remove the garlic and ginger pieces.

▸ Place broccoli, ½ cup flavoured cream, jalapeño, salt and pepper into a food processor and blend until a slightly creamy texture is achieved. If the mixture is too thick, add the remaining flavoured cream then set aside.

For the fish

▸ Mix the breadcrumbs and herbs together in a medium-sized bowl.

▸ Heat the olive oil and sauté the garlic and ginger. Add to the breadcrumb mixture.

▸ Mix the soy sauce and lemon juice together in a small bowl.

▸ Place the fish in a baking dish large enough to hold all 4 fillets in a single layer. Pour the soya mixture over the fish, ensuring that the fillets are well coated with the marinade.

▸ Set aside for 20 minutes, turning over the fillets after 10 minutes.

▸ Preheat the oven to 180°C (350°F).

▸ Spread the crumb mixture over the top of the fish fillets. Bake for 10–15 minutes.

To serve

▸ Heat the broccoli purée in the microwave and place a spoonful on each of 4 plates. Place a fish fillet on top of the purée and serve with braised carrots (master recipe, see p. 161) or a medley of grilled peppers.

Tilapia can be replaced with any flaky white fish such as hake.

This is a good recipe if you have an excess of broccoli in your garden or in your veggie box.

Spinach

Popeye's favourite vegetable has become one of my preferred greens in my adult life. I also discovered, since moving to South Africa, that it grows like a weed and is one that most Africans appreciate. Depending on where you live, there are different names for the varieties, such as morogo, spinach and even kale, though the end result is one of pure satisfaction.

Master recipe

Spinach and onion

MAKES 1½–2 CUPS

1 tablespoon olive oil	▶ Heat the oil in a large skillet or wok.
½ cup onion, chopped	▶ Sauté the onion until softened, then add the garlic and cook for a few minutes.
2 cloves garlic, minced	
8 cups shredded raw spinach	▶ Add spinach and cook until fully wilted. Season with nutmeg and salt and pepper.
2 pinches of grated nutmeg	
Sea salt and pepper to taste	▶ Serve as a side dish.

HEALTH BENEFITS

Spinach has a high fibre content, which helps to reduce blood sugar levels after a meal.

This leafy green is low in calories, high in vitamins A and K, as well as manganese and folate, which helps with maintaining bone, brain, skin and heart health.

Spinach is full of lutein and zeaxanthin, which are anti-oxidants that fight against age-related macular degeneration. Popeye must have also had great eyesight!

Beta-carotene, vitamins E and C and zinc are all found in spinach and serve to combat high blood pressure and osteoporosis.

BUYING AND STORING GUIDE

Look for vivid dark green, crisp leaves with healthy stalks.

Wash well to remove sand and wrap in paper towel before storing in the fridge.

Fresh spinach does not keep and must be eaten within a few days.

To freeze, remove leaves from stalks and blanch briefly in boiling water before transferring to ice water. Store in sealed containers in the freezer.

GREEN FINGERS

Spinach is typically a spring crop, but can continue into the summer if it is not too hot.

To pick spinach from your garden, cut the outer leaves first. This will allow the younger inner leaves to continue growing and will extend the growing season.

This green vegetable can easily grow in your garden or in a large pot so why not plant some with your fresh herbs.

Spinach and artichoke dip with pita chips

SERVES 6–8

Another way to utilise leftovers and cupboard staples that need to be used before the sell-by dates. I love making this quick dip when friends drop by.

Dip

1 cup cooked spinach
(master recipe, see p. 37)

½ cup sour cream

1 cup cream cheese

½ cup chopped grilled artichokes

¼ cup crumbled goat's cheese

1 tablespoon grated
Parmesan cheese

Pita chips

6 pita breads

½ cup olive oil

2 tablespoons sesame seeds

You need to keep a close watch on these chips while they are being grilled since they burn easily.

I use kitchen scissors to cut the pita into pieces. It is fast and efficient. Substitute dried herbs for the sesame seeds.

Dip

▸ Preheat the oven to 180°C (350°F).

▸ Mix all the ingredients, except the Parmesan cheese, together in a bowl.

▸ Fill an ovenproof dish with the mixture, sprinkle the top with Parmesan cheese and bake for 20 minutes.

▸ Serve hot with pita chips (see below) or crackers.

Pita chips

▸ Preheat the oven grill (broiler).

▸ Cut each pita into 6 wedges. Separate the top from the bottom of the pita wedges to make thin triangles.

▸ Place on a baking sheet. Brush with olive oil and sprinkle with sesame seeds.

▸ Bake under the grill until browned and crisp.

▸ If not using immediately, store in an airtight container. If they soften, just crisp up again in the oven.

Spanakopita cocktail triangles

MAKES 30 TRIANGLES

These triangles can be made in different sizes, depending on whether you are making them for a cocktail treat or a vegetarian luncheon. This is also a great recipe to make in bulk to keep in the freezer for surprise guests.

1 cup cooked spinach and onion (master recipe, see p. 37)

¼ cup crumbled feta

2 tablespoons chopped sun-dried tomatoes (packed in oil)

½ teaspoon lemon juice

Salt and pepper to taste

1 cup butter

10 phyllo sheets, thawed if frozen

1 tablespoon sesame seeds

▶ Preheat the oven to 180°C (350°F).

▶ Coarsely chop the spinach and onion mixture. Transfer to a bowl and stir in the feta, sun-dried tomatoes, lemon juice, salt and pepper.

▶ Melt the butter in a small saucepan, then allow to cool. It should remain runny.

▶ Cover the phyllo sheets with a dampened kitchen towel.

▶ Take 1 phyllo sheet and arrange on your work surface with the long side parallel to the counter's edge (keep remaining sheets covered).

▶ Brush the phyllo sheet with some of the melted butter. Top with another phyllo sheet and brush with more butter.

▶ Cut the buttered phyllo stack into 4 cm (2 in) wide strips that are perpendicular to the counter's edge.

▶ Place a heaped teaspoon of filling on the bottom of the strip, nearest to you. Fold a corner of phyllo to enclose the filling and form a triangle. Continue folding the strip (like a flag), maintaining triangular shape.

▶ Place the triangle, seam side down, on a large baking sheet covered with a silicone pad or baking paper. Brush the top with butter and sprinkle with sesame seeds.

▶ Make more triangles in the same manner, using all of phyllo and filling. Bake in the middle of the oven until golden brown, 20–25 minutes. Transfer to a rack to cool slightly.

Make sure that the filling is properly encased in the phyllo pastry, a bit like making a samosa.

I use a pizza cutter to cut the prepared phyllo sheets into strips, making life much easier.

Saag paneer

SERVES 4

This is one of my favourite Indian recipes. On a trip to India, I was taught not only how easy it is to make **saag** *(spinach) but also how easy it is to make paneer, the yummy cheese cubes in the spinach!*

Paneer

4 cups whole milk

1½ tablespoons white vinegar

Saag

2 cups cooked spinach
(master recipe, see p. 37)

1 tablespoon vegetable oil

1 tablespoon grated fresh ginger

½ cup chopped tomato

1 teaspoon turmeric

1 teaspoon chilli powder

A pinch of salt

1 cup water

½ teaspoon white pepper

Paneer

▸ Bring the milk to a boil, then take it off the heat and pour in the vinegar. Stir until it is curdled.

▸ Pour the mixture through a fine sieve. Place what is left in the sieve into a small, flat pan.

▸ Flatten the mixture until it is 2.5 cm (1 in) thick, making sure that it is well compacted so that it holds together.

▸ Cover with parchment paper, and then help to keep it well compacted by putting a brick (or something heavy) on top of it. Set aside for a few hours.

▸ This sounds harder than it really is!

Saag

▸ Before starting to cook, chop up 1 cup of spinach mixture in a food processor.

▸ Heat the oil in a medium saucepan. Add the ginger and fry until softened. Stir in the chopped tomato, turmeric, chilli, salt, both chopped and cooked spinach and water. Bring to a simmer while continuing to stir the mixture. Cook until most of the liquid has evaporated.

▸ While the spinach is simmering, cut the paneer into small squares.

▸ Heat oil in a skillet and gently place the paneer squares into the pan. Allow to brown then turn to fry the other side. Be gentle so that you do not crumble the paneer.

▸ Just before serving, add the paneer to the spinach mixture and gently combine.

▸ Season with a little white pepper and serve hot.

A good substitute for paneer that is easy to buy, cut and fry is halloumi.

The spinach is also good without the paneer if you are not feeling adventurous.

Spinach and ricotta gnocchi

SERVES 6 AS AN APPETIZER

I used to be afraid of making these Italian treats for fear of failing. It turns out that they are quite easy to make. Even if they do not look perfect, I can promise you they will taste great.

Gnocchi

1 cup cooked spinach
(master recipe, see p. 37)

1 cup fresh ricotta

1 cup grated Parmesan cheese

½ teaspoon grated nutmeg

2 egg yolks

1 teaspoon salt

½ teaspoon pepper

1 cup flour

extra 3 tablespoons grated
Parmesan cheese

Sage butter

3 tablespoons butter

16 fresh sage leaves

Gnocchi

▶ Chop up the spinach and remove all of the moisture by wrapping the spinach in a kitchen towel and twisting it.

▶ Place the ricotta, spinach, Parmesan, nutmeg and egg yolks in a large bowl. Mix until well combined. Season with salt and pepper.

▶ Using your hands, slowly incorporate ¾ cup of flour to create a slightly sticky dough.

▶ Divide the dough into 7 or 8 balls of equal size, then roll into long 2.5 cm (1 in) wide logs. Cut the logs into 3 cm (1.5 in) pieces with a lightly floured knife.

▶ Roll the back of a lightly floured fork over the gnocchi to create ridges and place on a baking sheet until ready to cook.

▶ Bring a large saucepan of water to a boil. Add a little salt and drop in half of the gnocchi, which will sink to the bottom. When they are ready (2–3 minutes), they will slowly rise to the surface of the simmering water.

▶ Using a slotted spoon, transfer the cooked gnocchi to a plate lined with paper towel. Cook the remaining gnocchi in the same way.

Sage butter

▶ In a large frying pan, heat the butter. Allow it to brown slightly before adding the sage leaves. Cook the sage leaves for 1 minute before adding the gnocchi.

▶ Stir until heated through and serve immediately in warm pasta bowls, with a sprinkling of Parmesan cheese.

These gnocchi are also ideal for freezing. Keep the raw gnocchi on a baking sheet, place in the freezer and, once frozen, transfer to an airtight container. They will keep for a few months in the freezer. Cook the gnocchi directly from the freezer though the cooking time will increase by a few minutes.

Zucchini

My husband has been the butt of many jokes when it comes to zucchini. Sadly, he is not a big veggie man and often brings home cucumbers instead of zucchinis. Over the years, I have had to create recipes that disguise this vegetable. I must admit that I have been surprisingly successful.

Grated zucchini

EAT IT NOW OR FREEZE IT FOR LATER

What to do with an excess of zucchini? The best is to grate and freeze it in 2-cup servings to be used in the recipes given here, as well as to keep as a handy stand-by for other dishes.

6 zucchini

3 sealable freezer bags

▶ If you want to eat it straight away, sauté half an onion in olive oil until translucent. Add the grated zucchini and continue cooking until softened. Add fresh summer herbs, such as thyme or basil, salt, pepper and a dollop of fresh cream. Serve warm with something off the grill.

HEALTH BENEFITS

Zucchini is beneficial in keeping cholesterol at bay because of its levels of fibre and vitamins C and A.

This green vegetable also has powerful anti-oxidants that are instrumental in reducing the risk of various cancers.

High in water and low in calories, zucchini is a great diet food. It is also believed to be a metabolism booster.

Did you know that zucchini has more potassium than a banana?

BUYING AND STORING GUIDE

Look for medium-sized, glossy and bright-skinned, green zucchini with no bruises or damp spots.

Remember, the darker the zucchini, the greater the amount of nutrients and minerals.

A late summer vegetable, zucchini can be stored for 3–5 days in the vegetable drawer of the fridge (some say wrapped in plastic, but I'm not a big plastic lover!).

GREEN FINGERS

Zucchini is a summer vegetable that can be grown in a container or the garden.

The more you pick, the longer the season.

There are male and female zucchini flowers. The female has a fruit (the zucchini itself) with the flower while the male has a single, bigger flower. This male flower is an Italian specialty that is stuffed and fried.

Zucchini plants like to soak up at least 6 hours of sun a day. They also enjoy a good water bath.

There is little waste with this vegetable since it is most often enjoyed with the skin on.

Zucchini bread

MAKES 1 LARGE LOAF

My daughter Charlotte used to take this bread to school for her midday pick-me-up. It became the snack of choice for the entire class. I was amazed by the daily orders I would receive from her classmates for this childhood treat of mine.

This recipe works equally well as a single loaf or as muffins, though the baking time would be reduced to 20 minutes for muffins.

3 eggs

1 cup castor sugar

1 cup vegetable oil

1 tablespoon vanilla essence

2 cups grated zucchini
(master recipe, see p. 47)

2 cups flour

1 tablespoon ground cinnamon

2 teaspoons bicarbonate of soda

¼ teaspoon baking powder

1 cup raisins or nuts (optional)

1 teaspoon salt

▸ Preheat the oven to 180°C (350°F). Grease a bread loaf tin.

▸ Beat the eggs in a medium-sized mixing bowl until frothy. Add the sugar, oil and vanilla and beat until thick and lemon-coloured.

▸ Add grated zucchini to the mixture.

▸ Sift the flour, cinnamon, bicarbonate of soda, baking powder and salt together in a separate bowl. Add the raisins or nuts, if using.

▸ Fold the dry ingredients into the zucchini-egg mixture. Pour the batter into the prepared tin and bake for 1 hour, or until fully cooked.

Frozen zucchini works well in this recipe though the moisture needs to be removed prior to using it by squeezing it in a kitchen towel.

Zucchini fritters

SERVES 4

This is a super-easy recipe that can be used for the basis of a main course or as an appetizer or a cocktail bite. It all depends on what size you decide to make these tasty little treats.

2 cups grated zucchini
(master recipe, see p. 47)

½ cup flour

½ teaspoon baking powder

¼ cup buttermilk

1 egg

1 tablespoon minced garlic

2 tablespoons minced fresh basil

1 tablespoon minced
fresh flat-leaf parsley

¼ cup crumbled Danish feta cheese

1 tablespoon olive oil

▸ Place the grated zucchini in a bowl and mix in the remaining ingredients.

▸ Heat an extra 2 tablespoons of vegetable oil in a skillet. Divide the batter into 4 patties and shallow-fry the fritters until browned on one side. Carefully flip over and cook the other side (5–8 minutes total).

▸ Place on a baking sheet. At this point, the fritters can be refrigerated for later use or finish cooking them in the oven at 180°C (350°F) for 10 minutes.

▸ Great topped with a salad of roasted tomato (see p. 119), chopped mozzarella and basil.

These fritters are easy to freeze for future use.

For those wanting gluten-free fritters, replace the flour with ¾ cup of rice flour.

Replace basil, parsley and olive oil with 2½ tablespoons pesto.

Zucchini bites

MAKES 18 MINI CUPS

This is a great way to use up leftover plain quinoa or even quinoa that has been prepared with flavourful herbs or minced vegetables. Add some egg, a little flour and some cheese and you cannot go wrong.

2 cups cooked quinoa

3 eggs

1 cup grated zucchini
(master recipe, see p. 47)

2 cloves garlic, minced

1 teaspoon dried thyme

a pinch of paprika

½ cup grated Emmenthal cheese

1 tablespoon flour

Salt and pepper to taste

▶ Preheat the oven to 180°C (350°F). Grease a mini-muffin pan.

▶ Combine all the ingredients in a large bowl.

▶ Fill the muffin cups to the top with the quinoa mixture. Bake for 15–20 minutes, or until a tester comes out clean.

▶ Serve with a dollop of crème fraîche mixed with a spoonful of sweet chilli sauce, a South African favourite.

Substitute chopped cooked spinach for the grated zucchini. Use rice flour for gluten-free bites.

I sometimes change the cheese to Cheddar.

Curried zucchini soup

SERVES 6

This is a wonderful soup that is quick to prepare and can be served with or without cream. If you need it to be thinned down, then add more vegetable stock.

1 tablespoon olive oil

1 large onion, chopped

1 tablespoon dried thyme

3 cups grated zucchini
(master recipe, see p. 47)

2 teaspoons curry powder (see
homemade curry powder on p. 181)

4 cups chicken or vegetable stock

Salt and pepper

1 cup heavy cream

▶ Heat the olive oil in a large saucepan and sauté the onion until translucent.

▶ Add the thyme and grated zucchini and cook until soft.

▶ Stir in the curry powder, and then add the stock and bring to a boil. Reduce the heat and simmer for 15 minutes.

▶ Purée the soup in a blender or use a stick blender. Season with salt and pepper to taste.

▶ Return the soup to the heat and stir in the cream until heated through. Serve with a Parmesan tuile (see below).

Parmesan tuile

▶ Create 4 mounds of grated parmesan cheese on a baking tray lined with a silicone mat or baking paper. Flatten the mounds to make 8 cm (4 in) diameter rounds. Bake in a preheated 200°C (400°F) oven until the cheese begins to melt and turn brown. They burn easily, so be vigilant. Remove from the oven and carefully lay the rounds over a rolling pin to give the half moon look. Allow to cool.

Avocado

Until arriving in South Africa, I had never considered that this fruit, not vegetable, could be seasonal. In most supermarkets in North America, avos are a staple. My whole family goes into mourning when these magical green treats disappear off menus and produce shelves here in Cape Town.

Master recipe

Avocado spread

SERVES 1

1 avocado, peeled and cubed

½ teaspoon fresh lemon juice

2 slices of toasted seed bread

Sea salt and pepper to taste

▸ With a knife, cut avocado in half, pit and cut into slices then into cubes.

▸ Mash the avocado and lemon juice together in a small bowl, using the back of a spoon. Spread on a piece of toasted seed bread.

▸ Sprinkle with sea salt and pepper and enjoy.

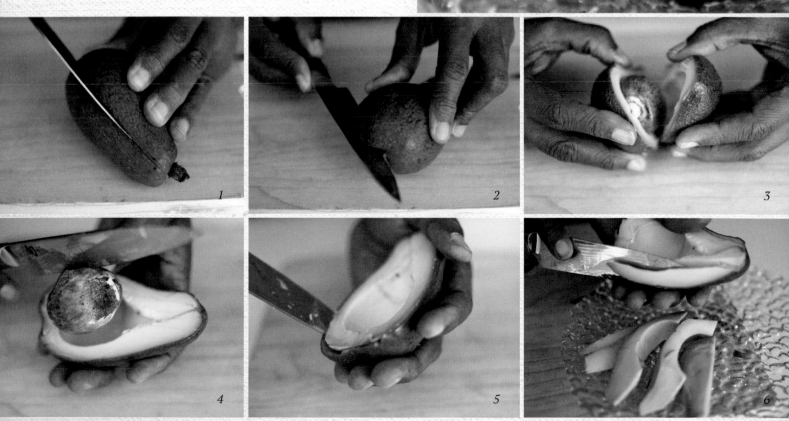

HEALTH BENEFITS

Avocados have high levels of anti-oxidants and folate, which help to prevent cancer and cardiovascular disease, and also reduce signs of aging.

Avocados have a higher level of potassium than bananas, and help to regulate blood pressure and prevent circulatory disease.

Avocados partner well with orange and red vegetables by helping with the absorption of beta-carotenes, which boost the immune system and helps in the fight against cancer.

Avocados have the highest protein content of any fruit.

BUYING AND STORING GUIDE

Look for slightly soft, heavy, firm, dark green avocados with no cracks or soft spots. A slight neck at the top of the fruit means that it was ripened on the tree.

Avocados ripen easily on the counter. Do not place them in the fridge unless you want to fully halt the ripening process.

To speed up the ripening process, wrap avocados with a tomato in a paper bag or newspaper.

Whole avocados can last up to a week in the fridge. Once cut open, they begin to brown immediately. Citrus juice sprinkled over the exposed flesh will counteract the oxidation process.

GREEN FINGERS

Avocados are related to laurel and cinnamon trees.

Stick 3 toothpicks around the middle part of the pit and suspend it in a container of water. Once the roots begin to grow, plant in soil in a sunny area. The tree will only fruit if the tree is pollinated.

Avocados do not fall off the tree when ripe so they can be left in "tree storage" for a long period of time.

Worms, pigs, chickens and compost heaps love avocado peels.

Avocado-apple smoothie

SERVES 2

Avocados are perfect companions to flavourful herbs such as coriander and, in this case, mint. If you decide to grow mint in your containers or garden, be sure to keep it contained since it grows like a weed.

1 ripe avocado, peeled and pit removed (master recipe, see p. 55)

½ Granny Smith apple

¼ cup low-fat plain yoghurt

½ cup apple juice or cider

1 tablespoon honey

juice of ½ lime

5 fresh mint leaves, or to taste

1 cup ice

▸ Combine all the ingredients in a blender, and blend until smooth.

▸ Serve in a tall glass with an apple slice and a few mint leaves to garnish.

To save half an avocado for future use, leave the pip intact, sprinkle lemon juice on the exposed surface and store well wrapped.

BBQ prawns with a spicy avocado sauce

SERVES 6

After visiting the Two Oceans aquarium in Cape Town, I have had to reduce my prawn consumption. Did you know that the by-catch from trawling prawns outweighs the actual catch 20 to 1 and farm-raised prawns have led to a 10% loss of the world's mangroves? I now appreciate every bite.

BBQ prawns

2 tablespoons vegetable oil

1 tablespoon minced garlic

1 tablespoon minced fresh ginger

1 tablespoon chilli powder

1 tablespoon soy sauce

18 queen (large) prawns, peeled and deveined

18 wooden skewers, soaked

3 tablespoons sweet chilli sauce, for serving

Spicy avocado sauce

4 large avocados, peeled and cubed (master recipe, see p. 55)

½ cup sour cream

1 ½ teaspoon prepared wasabi

1 tablespoon lemon juice

BBQ prawns

▶ Preheat the oven to 230°C (450°F) or fire up the barbecue.

▶ Mix the oil, garlic, ginger, chilli powder and soya sauce in a bowl. Rub this mixture all over the prawns and leave to marinate for 30 minutes.

▶ Arrange the prawns on an oiled baking sheet and bake for 5–7 minutes. If using the barbecue, thread the prawns onto skewers and grill over hot coals.

Spicy avocado sauce

▶ Mix all the sauce ingredients together in a bowl until well blended. Check for seasoning. Set aside for 30 minutes.

To serve

▶ Squeeze a small amount of sweet chilli sauce into a shot glass and top it with some avocado sauce. Place a prawn, on a skewer, into the glass. Serve three of these on a plate for each guest.

Save the prawn shells to make a quick fish stock (you can freeze them if you don't have time to make the stock immediately). Sauté the shells, then cover with water and simmer for a few minutes. Strain and save the stock for a paella or a chowder.

Avocado and smoked trout puff pastry rounds

SERVES 6

This is a great recipe to use up leftover store-bought puff pastry. If you do not have smoked trout then smoked salmon or cured salmon works just as well.

1 avocado, peeled and cubed (master recipe, see p. 55)

½ teaspoon lime juice

2 tablespoons crème fraîche

1 teaspoon prepared horseradish cream

½ packet ready-made puff pastry

4 pieces smoked trout, thinly sliced

Salt and pepper to taste

▸ Mash the avocado, and then add crème fraîche, lime juice, horseradish, salt and pepper. Refrigerate for 30 minutes.

▸ Preheat the oven to 180°C (350°F).

▸ Roll out the puff pastry as thinly as possible and cut out into small rounds about 5 cm (2 in) in diameter.

▸ Pierce little holes all over prepared pastry rounds, using a fork. Arrange on a baking sheet.

▸ Bake for 10 minutes, or until golden and slightly puffed. These are the bases for your avo and trout.

▸ Spread or pipe the avocado mixture onto the puff pastry bases.

▸ Create a rose with a small piece of trout and place on top of the avocado mixture.

▸ Add cracked pepper and a sprinkle of lime juice and serve.

Leftover puff pastry can be used to make cheese straws. Roll it out, sprinkle with a hard cheese and then fold the pastry over the cheese. Roll out again and then cut into strips. Twist the pastry strips, place on a baking sheet and bake at 200°C (400°F) for 10 minutes, or until golden brown.

BALT wrap

SERVES 2

*There is no better way to use up leftover avocado and bacon then in one of these wraps. To keep it vegetarian, remove the bacon and add any other vegetable you might have in the refrigerator.
To add an extra zing, add roquefort cheese to the avocado mixture.*

1 avocado, peeled and cubed (master recipe see p. 55)

½ teaspoon fresh lemon juice

¼ cup cream cheese

Sea salt and pepper to taste

1 tomato, sliced

6 pieces of crispy bacon

handful of mixed lettuce leaves

2 large tortilla wraps or 4 medium ones

▸ In a small bowl, mix together avocado, lemon juice, cream cheese and seasoning.

▸ Lay out both wraps on the counter and spread with the avocado mixture.

▸ Top with remaining ingredients and roll.

▸ Cut wrap on a diagonal and serve.

Kiwi

Once a New Zealand delicacy, this furry little vitamin C bomb has become a globetrotter. Whether you cut it in half and scoop out the flesh or bite right into it, the outcome is the same; a tart sweet surprise that envelopes your mouth with pure pleasure.

Master recipe
How to eat a kiwi

Slice and eat

▸ Keep the skin on and simply slice the washed fruit, removing the two ends.

Peel and slice or chop

▸ Starting at one end of the fruit, slowly peel the kiwi, going around the fruit.

Scoop and eat

▸ Cut the fruit in half then use a spoon to scoop out the sweet tasting flesh.

Decoration

▸ Use the kiwi as a decorative element on a plate, but be sure to use it afterwards. The flower look is created by inserting and removing the tip of a paring knife on a 45 degree angle into the kiwi, then again but in the opposite angle to create a circle of mini gnome hats. Once the circle is connected, the fruit will separate to create a kiwi flower.

There are so many ways to enjoy a kiwi and best of all you do not have to remove the skin. Here are a few pictures to help you navigate the preparation process.

HEALTH BENEFITS

The kiwi's high level of anti-oxidants has proven to be effective against age-related macular degeneration. It also boosts the immune system and fights against disease, including cancer.

With a high fibre count, kiwi is a must for the improved health of intestines, heart and blood.

Kiwi also increases energy levels due to its potassium and magnesium.

BUYING AND STORING GUIDE

When buying kiwi, look for ones that are plump, semi-firm and fragrant, without any visible soft spots or bruising.

Pair a kiwi with a banana or apple in a paper bag to speed up the ripening process. Be sure to remove it as soon as it is ripe since as it degenerates quickly.

Kiwi lasts up to 4 weeks in the fridge.

Kiwis have enzymes that act as protein busters, so only add to protein dishes just before serving.

GREEN FINGERS

Kiwis are grown on vines and need to remain dormant during winter to produce flowers, which in turn become fruits.

Bees are also needed in the kiwi growing cycle since they pollinate the flowers, which in turn enables the plant to develop fruits.

The growing cycle of a kiwi is 7 months.

The entire fruit, including the skin, can be eaten so no waste should be created from this fruit.

Baked salmon with a strawberry and kiwi cream

SERVES 6

Easy to prepare ahead of time and finish off at the last minute. The key is not to overcook the kiwi and strawberry mixture, otherwise it becomes mush.

> Salmon is best served slightly undercooked, so the centre is coral moving into a light pink on the outside.

1 cup whipping cream

24 red peppercorns

2 full salmon fillets, or enough for 6 people

1 tablespoon olive oil

Salt and pepper to taste

3 kiwis, peeled and cubed (master recipe, see p. 63)

24 medium strawberries, hulled and quartered

▸ Preheat the oven to 180°C (350°F).

▸ Combine cream and peppercorns in a small saucepan. Bring to a boil and allow to simmer for 5 minutes. Turn off the heat and allow the peppercorns to flavour the cream.

▸ Place the salmon fillets on a rimmed baking sheet (a silicone mat helps with clean up). Season with olive oil, salt and pepper.

▸ Place in the oven and bake until the centre is still coral. The timing depends on the size of the fish, but it should take 10–15 minutes. Once cooked, remove the fish from the oven.

▸ Reheat the cream, add the kiwis and strawberries and pour over the fish. Serve immediately.

Cocktail lamb koftas with a kiwi mint chutney

SERVES 6

These little meatballs can also be made into large kebabs, as I often do in the bush. The spices are reminiscent of the Indian influence in South African cuisine and the chutney is what all good South Africans love.

500 g (1 lb) lamb mince (ground)

3 cloves garlic, minced

1 teaspoon finely minced fresh ginger

1 tablespoon roasted pine nuts (can be done in the oven or on the stovetop)

1 teaspoon ground cumin*

1 teaspoon paprika*

1 teaspoon ground coriander*

2 teaspoons finely minced fresh mint

Sea salt and fresh ground black pepper

A pinch of chilli flakes

12 wooden skewers, soaked in water or wine/water mixture for 1 hour

2 tablespoons olive oil

▸ Mix the mince, garlic, ginger, pine nuts, spices, mint and chilli flakes in a large bowl and refrigerate for 1 hour.

▸ Shape the lamb mixture into bite-sized meatballs and cook in a frying pan with 2 tablespoons of oil or in the oven with a little less oil.

or

▸ Press the lamb mixture onto the skewers, into sausage shapes. Rub with oil and grill over hot coals, in a griddle pan or in the oven.

▸ Serve with kiwi chutney (see next page).

*For more flavour, use smoked paprika. Toast cumin and coriander seeds and then grind in a mortar and pestle or spice grinder.

Kiwi chutney

MAKES 1 CUP

2 teaspoons olive oil

¼ cup diced onion

1 large clove garlic, minced

1 cup peeled and diced kiwi fruit (master recipe, see p. 63)

½ cup dried blueberries and cranberries

½ teaspoon ground ginger

10 whole cloves

½ cup brown sugar

½ cup malt vinegar

▸ Heat the oil in a saucepan and sauté the onion and garlic until translucent but not browned.

▸ Add the kiwi, dried berries and spices. Cook until slightly softened but not mushy.

▸ Add the sugar and vinegar and mix well. Simmer until the dried fruits are plump and soft and the kiwi starts to lose shape (about 35 minutes). The vinegar should reduce to almost nothing and you will be left with a moist chutney.

▸ Serve with meatballs.

This chutney is also good on a toasted (grilled) Cheddar cheese sandwich.

Grilled honey-thyme chicken skewers with a kiwi and pineapple salsa

SERVES 6

This is a quick and easy dinner for family or unexpected guests. The fresh flavours of the salsa make this a perfect hot summer evening meal. You can warm up some tortilla shells and turn these skewers into chicken tacos with a little added sour cream and sliced avocado.

> *When making a salsa, be sure that all the ingredients are cut to the same size. You can also serve the chicken fillets whole.*

Chicken skewers

½ cup olive oil

¼ cup honey

1 teaspoon chilli powder

1 teaspoon dried thyme or 6 sprigs fresh thyme

6 skinless chicken breast fillets

6 wooden skewers, soaked in water or wine/water mixture for 1 hour

Kiwi and pineapple salsa

1 cup pineapple pieces, cut to match the size of other ingredients

3 kiwis, peeled and chopped (master recipe, see p. 63)

½ red onion, finely minced

½ jalapeño chilli pepper, seeded and chopped

½ orange pepper, chopped

2 tablespoons chopped fresh coriander

1 tablespoon chopped fresh mint

2 teaspoons lime juice

Kiwi and pineapple salsa

▶ Make the salsa first. Combine all the salsa ingredients in a bowl and toss gently. Refrigerate for at least 1 hour.

Chicken skewers

▶ Combine the olive oil, honey, chilli and thyme in a bowl.

▶ Flatten the chicken breasts and cut into long slices. Add the chicken pieces to the marinade and set aside for 30 minutes.

▶ Just before grilling, thread the chicken onto the skewers. Grill over medium-low heat, making sure that the honey marinade does not burn and char the breasts.

▶ Serve with the kiwi and pineapple salsa.

The norm for juleps is a silver drinking cup but a glass will do in a pinch.

Kiwi and mint julep

SERVES 4

I was introduced to mint juleps by a friend in Kentucky who used to host the best Derby parties, fried chicken and all. I am not a big bourbon fan so the addition of kiwi softens the drink and makes it a very pleasant libation.

4 peeled and chopped kiwis (master recipe, see p. 63)

2 teaspoons lime juice

1 cup prepared mint simple syrup

4 cups ice cubes

4 jiggers bourbon

4 metal cups

4 fresh mint leaves, for garnishing

Mint simple syrup

½ cup sugar

1 cup water

¼ cup fresh mint leaves, removed from stalk

▸ Place the kiwis, lime juice, syrup (without the mint leaves), bourbon and ice cubes in a blender. Crush the mixture together and pour into individual cups.

▸ Garnish with a mint leaf and serve immediately.

Mint simple syrup

▸ Bring the water and sugar to a boil in a small saucepan.

▸ After 2 minutes of boiling, take the saucepan off the heat and drop in the mint leaves. Stir and let sit overnight to create a flavourful mint simple syrup.

▸ Before using the syrup, remove the mint leaves.

Simple syrup is the basis of a lot of cocktails so it is great to have it on hand in the fridge.

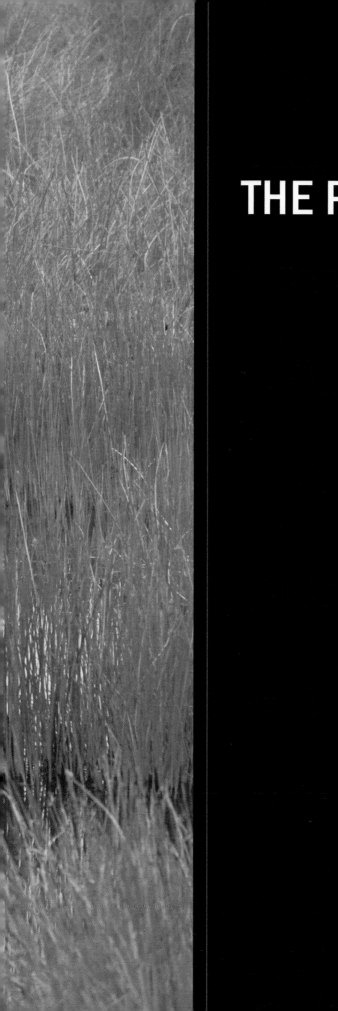

THE PURPLES

A Maribou stork out for a stroll near Selinda Căamp, Selinda Spillway, Botswana

Red cabbage

Red cabbage is another very popular vegetable here in South Africa. It is relatively easy to grow, though once you pick the beautiful round ball of goodness, it is over for the season. I have learned to share my cabbages with my friends. We either make salads or cook them into winter sweet-and-sour delicacies.

Master recipe

Red cabbage salad

SERVES 6

4 cups shredded red cabbage

2 cups cored and julienned
Granny Smith apples

½ red onion, thinly sliced

2 tablespoons white
balsamic vinegar

¼ cup olive oil

1 teaspoon honey

Sea salt and pepper to taste

▸ Mix all the ingredients together
in a medium-sized bowl, and
set aside for 30 minutes before
serving.

*To reduce the strength
of red onions, soak the
slices in a bowl of white
vinegar for 10 minutes,
rinse and use.*

HEALTH BENEFITS

High in anti-oxidants, cabbage has impressive anti-inflammatory, anti-cancer and anit-dimentia properties.

Cabbage is an excellent source of essential vitamins and minerals including vitamins C, K and A, which helps maintain healthy eyes and skin.

It is also a very good source of fibre, manganese and folate, which are imperative for a strong digestive system.

Cooked or raw cabbage has valuable cholesterol-reducing effects on the human body due to its fibre-related nutrients.

BUYING AND STORING GUIDE

Choose heads of cabbage that are heavy and firm with shiny. colourful leaves and robust stems. If the stems are cracking, the cabbage is old.

Cabbage will keep for two weeks in the fridge.

Cabbage can be shredded, blanched, cooled and frozen for future use.

When growing cabbage, the excess can be stored by hanging them from their stems in a cool, dark place such as a cellar or a cool garage.

Pre-cut cabbage loses most of its vitamin C content so it is best to buy it whole.

When cooking red cabbage, some sort of acid needs to be added to preserve the rich, purple colour of the vegetable.

GREEN FINGERS

Cabbage is a hardy vegetable that can be grown in the garden as well as in pots or flower boxes. The key is not to let it dry out.

Cabbage is considered the oldest recorded vegetable. It is part of the cruciferous or brassica family.

Cabbage does not like to be planted near strawberries, tomatoes or dill.

Remember to be careful when using a blender and hot liquid. It expands so only fill the jug half full with hot soup mixture or allow to cool before puréeing.

Cabbage and apple soup shooters

MAKES 10–12 SHOOTERS OR 6 BOWLS

This soup could be served hot or cold. This is a great way to use up leftover cabbage salad, and the apple adds a lovely crisp taste.

2 tablespoons butter

½ cup finely diced onion

1 teaspoon caraway seeds

2½ cups red cabbage salad (master recipe, see p. 73)

4 cups vegetable or chicken stock

½ cup fresh apple cider or juice

2 tablespoons apple cider vinegar

1 tablespoon dark brown sugar

Sea salt and ground black pepper

½ cup whipping cream

½ green apple, cored and thinly sliced

▶ Melt the butter in a large saucepan over medium-low heat.

▶ Add the onion and sweat until soft and translucent. Add the caraway seeds and stir for an additional minute.

▶ Add the cabbage salad and stir to combine.

▶ Increase the heat and continue cooking for a few minutes, until the cabbage softens.

▶ Pour in the stock, cider, vinegar and sugar. Bring to a boil, then reduce the heat. Cover and simmer for 30 minutes.

▶ Allow the mixture to cool before using a stick blender to purée the soup. Purée the soup in batches, if using a blender.

▶ Return the soup to the saucepan and check for seasoning. Stir in ¼ cup of the cream

▶ Serve with some sliced apple and a swirl of cream.

Sweet-and-sour red cabbage

SERVES 4

A Hungarian friend of mine introduced me to sweet-and-sour cabbage when she made it for me for our 10th wedding anniversary dinner. It goes beautifully with crispy duck or duck breast.

1 tablespoon olive oil

1 onion, peeled and sliced

3 cups red cabbage salad (master recipe, see p. 73)

½ cup balsamic vinegar

2 tablespoons brown sugar

Sea salt and freshly ground black pepper

1 tablespoon chopped fresh parsley

▸ Heat the olive oil in a saucepan and sauté the onion for a few minutes until soft and golden.

▸ Add the cabbage salad, balsamic vinegar and sugar and stir until well combined. Replace the lid and continue to cook over low heat for 30 minutes, checking and stirring every so often.

▸ Season with salt and pepper and stir in the parsley.

▸ Serve warm as an accompaniment to duck.

Asian chicken salad

SERVES 4–6

This is a great way to use up leftover roast chicken if you do not want to cook the chicken breasts. I love the refreshing Asian flavours.

2 cups red cabbage salad (master recipe, see p. 73)

½ cup julienned carrots

⅓ cup diagonally sliced spring onions

1 teaspoon plus 3 tablespoons soy sauce

3½ teaspoons sugar

Sea salt

1 clove garlic

2.5 cm (1 in) piece fresh ginger, peeled and sliced

¼ cup packed coriander leaves

3 tablespoons creamy peanut butter

1 tablespoon lemon juice

2 tablespoons peanut oil

4 chicken breast fillets, sliced (or a roasted chicken from the supermarket)

1 tablespoon chopped fresh coriander

⅓ cup roasted chopped peanuts

▸ In a large bowl, combine the cabbage salad, carrots, spring onions, 1 teaspoon soy sauce, 1 teaspoon sugar, and a big pinch of salt. Set aside for 20 minutes, tossing occasionally.

▸ Chop the garlic and ginger in a food processor. Scrape the bowl with a spatula, add the ¼ cup coriander leaves and chop thoroughly.

▸ Scrape the bowl and add the peanut butter, 1 tablespoon hot water, the lemon juice, 1 tablespoon peanut oil, and the remaining soy sauce and sugar. Pulse until well combined, scraping the bowl as needed.

▸ In a large skillet over medium-high heat, heat the remaining peanut oil. Season the chicken pieces with salt and put them in the hot pan (in batches, if necessary). Cook on one side until the edges are white (1–2 minutes); turn and cook until just firm, another 1–2 minutes.

▸ Transfer to a cutting board and stack the chicken in one or two piles; rest for 3–4 minutes. Slice the chicken into generous 5 mm (¼ in) strips and put them in a large bowl. Squeeze the cabbage mixture to remove excess moisture and add the cabbage to the chicken. Pour in the dressing and toss well to combine.

▸ Divide the salad among four plates and garnish with the remaining coriander and the roasted peanuts.

Fish tacos with cumin-scented cucumber and cabbage slaw

SERVES 4

I love fish tacos and all the wonderful fillings you can add to make it your own. This is a great way to throw an informal party, where everyone can add their favourite fillings to create their own signature dish.

12 small tortilla shells

Cabbage

2 cups red cabbage salad (master recipe, see p. 73)

1 tablespoon chopped fresh coriander

½ fresh jalapeño chilli pepper, minced

Sour cream

½ cup sour cream

1 teaspoon lemon juice

Cucumber salad

1 English cucumber

2 tablespoons rice vinegar

2 teaspoons mirin

½ teaspoon cumin seeds

½ teaspoon sea salt

Salmon

1 tablespoon vegetable oil

½ teaspoon ground cumin

¼ teaspoon chilli powder

½ lb (225 g) salmon fillet

For the cabbage

▸ In a small bowl, mix the cabbage salad with the coriander and jalapeño and set aside.

For the sour cream

▸ In a small bowl, mix the sour cream and lemon juice together.

For the cucumber salad

▸ Mix the rice vinegar, mirin, cumin and salt together in a medium-sized bowl.

▸ Peel the cucumber and create long slices using a vegetable peeler. Add to the mirin mixture and set aside for 30 minutes.

For the salmon

▸ Preheat the oven to 200°F (400°F).

▸ In a small bowl, mix the vegetable oil with the cumin and chilli powder.

▸ Place the fish fillet in a roasting pan and brush with seasoned oil.

▸ Either grill or broil the fish for 10–15 minutes, or until cooked through.

▸ To create your own taco, take a little of each filling, place in a tortilla shell and eat with delight.

Eggplant

Eggplants come in different shapes and sizes and remain the most difficult vegetable to sell to my family. I have learned, over the years, to disguise this purple gem in various recipes and they are finally beginning to appreciate the redeeming qualities of this summer vegetable.

Master recipe

Roasted eggplant

SERVES 3–4 AS A SIDE DISH

2 medium Italian globe eggplants

1 tablespoon salt

2 tablespoons olive oil

▶ Slice the eggplants into
2.5 cm (1 in) thick slices and
sprinkle with salt.

▶ Set aside for 30 minutes on a
baking sheet.

▶ Preheat the oven to 200°C
(400°F).

▶ Wipe off excess moisture and
return to baking sheet.

▶ Brush with olive oil and place in
the oven until cooked through
and slightly brown.

▶ Enjoy with a dollop of tzatziki and
some grilled lamb skewers.

HEALTH BENEFITS

The high fibre content of eggplants helps to maintain a healthy digestive tract and colon. They are also ideal to eat as an appetizer since the fibre helps to create a feeling of fullness and reduces the need to overeat.

Eggplant, especially the skin, is full of anti-oxidants, which helps to reduce the risk of cancer as well as bad cholesterol and viruses.

Eggplants contain a lot of water, just like the human body, so they are important, especially if eaten raw, in helping to retain healthy skin and hair.

Depending on the variety of eggplant, look for a smooth, shiny skinned vegetable with a green stem.

To test the ripeness of an eggplant, gently press your thumb pad into the skin. If it springs back, then it is ripe and perfect for cooking.

Eggplants last for up to a week in the fridge. If the skin is damaged, the eggplant will begin to rot. Brown spots are the first sign of decay.

If you have an abundance of eggplants, consider salting, flash-frying and freezing slices in containers. The consistency changes slightly, but is still excellent to use in cooked dishes. Slices can also be breaded, fried and frozen.

GREEN FINGERS

Eggplants belong to the nightshade family, which includes the tomato bush.

Eggplants grow on bushes. They initially begin as small purple flowers that bloom into large oblong, purple globes.

Eggplants are easy to grow and can be planted in a garden or in a planter on a balcony.

Tanzanian eggplant curry

SERVES 4

After visiting Zanzibar and its various spice markets, I could not help but create a curry dish from this country. The use of spices, coconut milk and eggplant was just too good to resist. This is a great option for a vegetarian meal, served with rice.

2 tablespoons olive oil

½ cup minced onions

2 cloves garlic, minced

1 tablespoon minced ginger

1 teaspoon curry powder (see p. 181)

3 cups roasted eggplant (4 small raw)
(master recipe, see p. 81)

1½ cups roasted tomatoes (450 g/1 lb raw)
(master recipe, see p. 119)

¾ cup coconut milk

Sea salt and freshly ground pepper to taste

¼ cup shredded coconut, toasted

1 tablespoon chopped fresh coriander

▶ Heat the olive oil in a medium-sized frying pan and sauté the onion until soft.

▶ Add the garlic and ginger and continue cooking for a few minutes. Add the curry powder and cook until aromatic, 3–5 minutes.

▶ Add the eggplant and tomatoes and continue cooking until well combined and heated through.

▶ Pour in the coconut milk and cook for a few more minutes. Season with salt and pepper to taste.

▶ Just before serving, sprinkle with toasted coconut and coriander.

▶ Serve with basmati rice.

Eggplant caponata

SERVES 4–6

This Mediterranean dish is one of my favourites because it is so versatile. It can be served as an appetizer, as a filling for an omelette, or as a topping to grilled fish the following day.

1 tablespoon olive oil

½ cup finely diced onion

½ cup seeded and chopped tomatoes

½ cup diced red bell pepper

2 tablespoons finely chopped Kalamata olives

2 tablespoons capers, drained and chopped

2 tablespoons raisins

2 tablespoons pine nuts, lightly roasted

2 cups roasted eggplant, cut into bite-sized cubes (master recipe, see p. 81)

2 tablespoons red wine vinegar

1 tablespoon chopped fresh parsley

Salt and pepper

▶ Heat the oil in a skillet over medium heat and sauté the onion for 3 minutes. Add the tomatoes, red bell pepper, olives, capers, raisins and pine nuts.

▶ Cook, covered, for 5 minutes, or until all the ingredients are heated through. Add the eggplant and cook for 2–3 minutes more until the flavours have blended. Stir in the vinegar followed by the parsley. Season to taste with salt and pepper.

This can be served as topping on bruschetta or as an accompaniment to grilled fish or chicken.

Keep pine nuts frozen in the freezer to last longer.

Pine nuts are easily dry-roasted by placing them in a skillet over medium heat and allowing them to brown. Keep a constant eye on them and stir regularly until the proper colour is achieved.

Eggplant and lentils

SERVES 6

This recipe uses all of the summer Mediterranean vegetables that are easily grown in a veggie garden. You can vary the vegetables depending on what you have in the fridge or garden.

1 cup roasted eggplant (master recipe, see p. 81), cut into bite-sized cubes

½ medium red onion, thinly sliced

2 medium tomatoes diced

½ cup minced yellow bell peppers

1 cup dried green or brown lentils, cooked

¼ cup crumbled feta cheese

1 tablespoon chopped fresh coriander

extra coriander, for garnishing

Lemon and honey vinaigrette

1 tablespoon lemon juice

2 tablespoons olive oil

1 tablespoon honey

Sea salt and pepper to taste

▸ In a medium bowl, mix the eggplant, onion, tomatoes, bell peppers, lentils, feta and coriander together.

▸ In a small bowl, whisk the lemon juice, olive oil, honey, salt and pepper together.

▸ Pour the vinaigrette over the salad and serve garnished with sprigs of coriander.

For those who do not eat coriander, like my friend Brigitte, you can use parsley.

Crumbled soft French goat's cheese also works in this recipe.

Mini eggplant and caramelized onion strudel

SERVES 6

These strudels can be served as a lunch item with a green salad or made into small parcels and served as hors d'oeuvres. Either way they are full of flavour and great to have ready-made in the freezer.

¼ cup olive oil

3 large onions, finely sliced

¼ cup brown sugar

2 cups roasted eggplant (master recipe, see p. 81), cut into bite-sized cubes

400 g (14½ oz) can, chopped peeled tomatoes, drained

4 sprigs of fresh thyme

2 tablespoons crumbled goat's cheese

Coarse salt and coarsely ground black pepper

12 sheets of phyllo pastry

Olive oil spray or olive oil for brushing

1 tablespoon sesame seeds

▸ Preheat the oven to 180°C (350°F).

▸ Heat the oil in a skillet over medium to low heat and soften the onions with the lid on.

▸ Stir in the sugar and continue cooking without a lid for another 10 minutes.

▸ Add the eggplant and drained tomatoes.

▸ Sprinkle with thyme and cook, uncovered, for another 20 minutes until the mixture is very dry. Stir once in a while.

▸ Mix in the goat's cheese and season with salt and pepper.

▸ Brush 4 sheets of phyllo pastry with olive oil. Stack them one on top of the other.

▸ Cut the stacked sheets in half. Repeat with the remaining phyllo pastry.

▸ Add a heaped tablespoon of mixture in the centre and at the bottom of each phyllo half.

▸ Fold in the sides and roll up each half to make individual strudels.

▸ Brush with oil and sprinkle with sesame seeds.

▸ Place on a baking sheet and bake for 30 minutes, or until golden brown.

When brushing with olive oil, use very little, otherwise the phyllo will be very oily when baked.

A pizza cutter works well to cut the phyllo pastry.

To make hors d'oeuvre-sized strudels, cut the phyllo into more strips to make much smaller parcels.

The uncooked strudels can be frozen and baked at a later date.

Blueberry

Having grown up in one of the blueberry growing regions of the world, it is hard for me not to love these mind-strengthening purple berries. The wild ones are by far the best, but the larger, juicy ones are also an acceptable second.

Blueberries and yoghurt

SERVES 4

2 cups blueberries, washed

1 cup Greek yoghurt

2 tablespoons brown sugar

2 tablespoons shelled pistachios

▶ Place a spoonful of blueberries in individual glasses.

▶ Top with a dollop of yoghurt, a sprinkle of brown sugar and ½ tablespoon of pistachios.

▶ Serve for breakfast or a light luncheon dessert.

BUYING AND STORING GUIDE

HEALTH BENEFITS

Blueberries are considered a super fruit due to their anti-oxidant super powers.

This fruit is associated with fighting cancer cells as well as having anti-inflammatory properties to help in the fight against ageing and heart disease. It also promotes brain health.

Blueberries are full of vitamins C, A and E, as well as dietary fibre.

Blueberries are from the same family as cranberries and help in the restoration of urinary tract health.

The carotenoids found in blueberries are helpful in the prevention of and delay in the development of eye disease.

Look for blueberries that have a deep, intense colour. Be sure that there is no mould growing in the bunch as a little mould multiplies very quickly.

Blueberries are sturdy and can be stored in their container as long as the damaged or mouldy berries have been removed. If the containers holding the berries are already stained, then the berries have already begun to rot and it is best not to buy them.

Only wash blueberries just prior to using them. If refrigerated immediately after being picked, the blueberries will last a week or so.

To store an over-abundance of blueberries, freeze in a single layer on a baking sheet. Once frozen, transfer to a bag and seal for future use.

GREEN FINGERS

If picking your own berries, the most effective technique is to choose a bunch, rub the fruit between your fingers and the ripe ones will fall into the waiting bucket.

For the best berries, pick in the early morning before the temperatures become too hot and the berries become too soft.

Blueberries grow on a bush and belong to the heath family. Other members of the heath family include cranberries, azaleas and rhododendrons.

Lemon blueberry cake squares

SERVES 6-8

This is a wonderful tea cake or luncheon cake that is a delightful combination of lemon tartness and bursts of blueberries that are a reminder of summer. Surplus blueberries can be frozen to be used later in the year for this cake.

1½ cups flour

1 teaspoon baking powder

½ teaspoon salt

3 eggs

1 cup castor sugar

½ cup vegetable oil

1 cup plain yoghurt

1 teaspoon vanilla essence

2 teaspoons lemon zest

1 tablespoon lemon juice

1 cup blueberries

▶ Preheat the oven to 180°C (350°F). Grease a 18 x 18 cm (7" x 11") baking pan.

▶ Sift the flour, baking powder and salt together in a small bowl.

▶ Cream the eggs and sugar together in a medium-sized bowl. Once the egg mixture is light yellow and frothy, mix in the oil followed by the yoghurt, vanilla, lemon zest and juice.

▶ Fold in the flour mixture, being careful not to over mix. Gently fold in the blueberries so as not to squish them.

▶ Pour the mixture into the prepared pan. Bake for 40–45 minutes, or until a wooden skewer inserted into the centre of the cake comes out clean.

If someone does not finish their blueberries and yoghurt (master recipe, see p. 89) then transform the extra glasses into this wonderful cake. Be sure to measure correctly.

Blueberry martini

SERVES 2–4, DEPENDING ON SIZE OF MARTINI GLASS

The base of this martini is a blueberry sauce, which can also be enjoyed with ice cream or as a topping on crêpes or pancakes.

Blueberry sauce

1 cup blueberries

¼ cup sugar

1 teaspoon lemon juice

▸ Place the blueberries, sugar and lemon juice in a small saucepan and cook over medium heat for 10 minutes. Once the blueberries start bursting, remove from the heat and allow to cool.

▸ Purée the mixture in a blender.

Martini

⅔ cup lemon-flavoured vodka

1 cup cranberry juice

¼ cup blueberry sauce

splash of triple sec

▸ Place 4–5 small ice cubes in martini glasses.

▸ Pour the vodka, cranberry juice, blueberry sauce and triple sec into a shaker filled with ice. Replace the top and shake well.

▸ Remove the ice from the glasses and pour the martini mixture into the cooled glasses.

▸ Garnish with a lemon peel twisted around a blueberry on a toothpick.

Freeze leftover blueberry sauce in an ice-cube tray to be used with a blueberry ice tea, or keep for a sauce on vanilla ice cream when you are looking for a quick dessert.

Blueberry clafouti

SERVES 8

This is a quick and easy French country dessert to make with staple kitchen ingredients. Depending on the occasion, this recipe can be made into individual servings or served in a large pie plate.

1 cup flour

⅔ cup castor sugar

4 eggs

1½ cups milk

1 teaspoon vanilla essence

1 tablespoon castor sugar, for coating

3 cups blueberries

2 teaspoons butter, melted

2 teaspoons icing sugar, for dusting

▸ Preheat the oven to 180°C (350°F).

▸ Rinse the blueberries and leave to dry.

▸ Sift the flour and castor sugar into a medium-sized bowl.

▸ In another medium-sized bowl, beat the eggs, milk and vanilla together.

▸ Pour the wet ingredients into the dry ingredients and carefully mix together until the batter is smooth.

▸ Lightly butter 8 individual tart dishes and coat lightly with castor sugar, shaking off any excess.

▸ Arrange the blueberries to cover the base of the dishes and pour the batter over them.

▸ Bake for 20–25 minutes, or until the clafoutis are puffed, set and golden brown.

▸ Remove from the oven, dust with icing sugar and serve hot with whipped cream.

This dessert is also good served at room temperature for lunch or a picnic.

Blueberry, corn and cucumber salad

SERVES 6

This is a summer favourite combining many of the typical Canadian summer flavours in one bowl. When I found this recipe in the June 2010 issue of Better Homes and Gardens, *I had to share it with friends and family. It is surprisingly refreshing and easy to prepare for a quick salad to compliment grilled meat.*

6 ears sweet corn (master recipe p. 169)

1½ cups blueberries

4 baby cucumbers, cut into bite-sized quarters

¼ large red onion, finely sliced

¼ cup chopped fresh coriander

Sea salt and freshly ground pepper

Chilli and lime vinaigrette

1 small red chilli pepper, seeded and finely chopped

2 tablespoons lime juice

2 tablespoons olive oil

1 tablespoon honey

½ teaspoon ground cumin

▸ Cut the corn kernels off the cobs.

▸ Place the corn, blueberries and chopped cucumbers in a bowl.

▸ Add the red onion and chopped coriander and toss gently.

▸ Season with salt and pepper.

▸ In a separate bowl, whisk all the dressing ingredients together.

▸ Once emulsified, pour the vinaigrette over the salad.

▸ Set aside for 30 minutes before serving so that the flavours blend.

The corn cobs can be saved and stored in the freezer and later used to flavour corn chowder.

For a bird treat during the cold northern winter months, remove a couple of cobs from the freezer, cover in peanut butter and roll in any seeds you have in the cupboard. Hang on a string out in the garden.

Plum

There is such a large variety of plums available that I am constantly trying to find ways to capture the myriad of flavours long after the final summer bounty has been collected.

Poached plums

SERVES 6

1½ cups white wine (or red wine)

½ cup sugar

1 cinnamon stick

rind of ½ orange, thinly sliced with white pith removed

6 medium plums
(approx. 1lb/500g),
halved and pitted

▸ Pour the wine and sugar into a medium saucepan. Heat over medium heat until all the sugar has dissolved. Add the cinnamon stick, orange rind and plums.

▸ Simmer over medium to low heat for 10–15 minutes. The plums need to give easily when poked with a fork, but should not be mushy.

▸ Transfer the plums to a bowl using a slotted spoon and allow to cool.

▸ Continue simmering the cooking liquid until it thickens and becomes a syrup. If it coats the back of a spoon, it is ready.

▸ Pour the cooled liquid over the plums and refrigerate. Do not let the plums sit in hot liquid otherwise they will become mushy.

▸ Serve over ice cream for a light, summery dessert.

HEALTH BENEFITS

Did you know that a prune is a dried plum? Just like its dried counterpart, plums can also stimulate bowel movements if you keep the skin on.

Plums are full of free radicals, creating a good line of defense against cancer.

Plums are a good source of vitamins A, C and E, as well as iron, calcium, magnesium, fibre and potassium.

BUYING AND STORING GUIDE

Plums belong to the stone fruit group and are ripe when you squeeze the fruit and it gives a little.

Ripe plums are best stored in the fridge for 3–5 days.

This fruit needs to be enjoyed in season or made into a jam since it cannot be frozen for future use.

GREEN FINGERS

Did you know that prior to modern farming methods, plums used to be dried on trees in the sun to wrinkle up like raisins and become prunes.

There are many different types of plums and they come in various colours, sizes and levels of sweetness.

Plum trees flower in the spring, are pollinated by bees and give fruit in the summer. They are deciduous trees and lose their leaves in the fall.

Like a peach, plum stones can be collected, dried in the oven and used as decorative soil cover for plotted plants.

Spiced duck breasts with poached plums

SERVES 2

Duck breasts are simple to prepare and are often paired with some sort of fruit sauce. This is a good basic recipe for cooking duck breast; you can create other fruit sauces if you feel daring.

2 duck breasts, skin on and scored

sea salt and freshly ground black pepper

1 teaspoon olive oil

1 teaspoon Chinese five-spice powder

¼ cup plum poaching liquid (master recipe, see p. 97)

1 tablespoon orange juice

½ teaspoon orange zest

½ red chilli pepper, finely chopped

½ cup chicken stock

2 poached plums (master recipe, see p. 97), chopped

4 sprigs of thyme

▶ Season the duck with sea salt and freshly ground black pepper, then rub with the olive oil and Chinese five-spice.

▶ Place a frying pan over medium-high heat. Once hot, fry the duck, skin-side down, for 5–6 minutes, or until the skin is brown and crisp.

▶ Turn the duck over and cook for a further 2–3 minutes, until cooked but still pink in the middle.

▶ Transfer the duck to a warm plate and set aside to rest. Reserve any of the pan juices for the sauce.

▶ Pour the plum poaching liquid, orange juice, orange zest, chopped chilli and chicken stock into the reserved pan. Bring the liquid to a boil and boil briskly for 5 minutes.

▶ Add the duck to the sauce as well as the plum pieces and 2 thyme sprigs. Continue cooking for another 3–4 minutes until the plums are heated through.

▶ Plate the duck and serve with the sauce. Garnish with the remaining sprigs of thyme.

Poached plum tea cakes

MAKES 8 TARTS

These tasty little tea cakes were one of my favorite go to recipes to prepare in game reserves for the snack before the afternoon game drive. The plums can easily be replaced with other fruit found laying about in the kitchen.

¾ cup flour

¼ cup almond flour

½ teaspoon baking powder

¼ teaspoon bicarbonate of soda

¼ cup salted butter, softened

¾ cup sugar

1 egg

½ cup buttermilk

4 poached plum halves (master recipe, see p. 97), sliced

1 teaspoon icing sugar

- ▸ Preheat the oven to 350°F (180°C).
- ▸ Butter and lightly flour 4 individual fluted cake moulds.
- ▸ Mix together both flours, the baking powder and bicarbonate of soda.
- ▸ In a separate bowl, cream the butter and sugar together until pale yellow. Beat in the egg.
- ▸ Add flour mixture to the butter mixture in two batches, alternating with the buttermilk. Be sure not to overmix.
- ▸ Pour the batter into the prepared cake moulds, to three-quarters full. Gently place the plum slices over the top.
- ▸ Bake in a preheated oven for 20–25 minutes until lightly browned and springy to the touch.
- ▸ Allow the cakes to cool before dusting with icing sugar.

2 pork tenderloins

Marinade

1 tablespoon minced garlic

1 thumbnail-sized piece of fresh ginger, grated

¼ cup soy sauce

¼ cup vegetable oil

1 star anise

Poached plum butter

6 poached plum halves (master recipe, see p. 97)

½ cup poaching liquid

Marinade

▸ Combine the garlic, ginger, soy sauce, oil and star anise and pour over the pork tenderloins. Marinate for a few hours.

Poached plum butter

▸ To make the butter, place the plums and poaching liquid in a small saucepan. Bring to a boil and then reduce the heat to low, keeping the pan covered. Allow the plums to dissolve into a lumpy sauce. Continue to stir regularly to reduce the mixture to a jammy butter. This could take up to an hour of checking and stirring every 5–10 minutes.

▸ Heat a griddle pan or the grill. Remove the tenderloins from the marinade and cook for 8–10 minutes per side. Be careful not to burn the meat. Set aside for a few minutes before serving to allow the juices to settle.

To serve

▸ Carve the tenderloin into slices and serve with the plum butter on the side.

Grilled pork tenderloin with poached plum butter

SERVES 6

Pork and plum make the perfect pair. The sweetness of the plum butter works beautifully with a grilled piece of pork. This butter is very versatile and can also be enjoyed with a toasted baguette or seed bread.

If you do not have poached plums, cut some fresh plums in half, grill them alongside the pork and serve without a sauce.

THE REDS

Smiling hippo at Jacana camp,
Okavango Delta, Botswana.

Beetroot

This root vegetable is another South African favourite that seems to be on every menu. Though it is not a favourite of any of my family members, I grow this trusty vegetable in my garden to satisfy my culinary cravings. I also love the colour it adds to any recipe.

Master recipe

Baked beetroot

Ingredients	Method
12 beetroot	▶ Preheat the oven to 200°C (400°F).
1–2 tablespoons red wine vinegar, depending on the size of the beetroot	▶ Wash the beetroot and trim the stalks, but keep the tip and tail intact to prevent 'bleeding'. Wrap 1–2 beetroot of similar size separately in foil and place on a baking sheet.
1 teaspoon sea salt	▶ Bake for 40–50 minutes, or until the beetroot are fork tender.
	▶ Allow beetroot to cool slightly before removing skin using two old towels, one to hold the beetroot and the other to rub off the skin. Slice, drizzle with red wine vinegar and salt to serve.

If you decide to boil your beetroot, be sure to reserve the beet water to drink or use in a soup. The many beet benefits are in that water.

HEALTH BENEFITS

Beetroot is rich in folate, which is beneficial during pregnancy.

The fibre found in beetroot contributes to reducing the risk of heart disease.

A good source of vitamin C, beetroot helps to build up a strong immune system while also reducing the occurrence of asthma.

The presence of beta-carotene in beetroot helps to strengthen eyes and the brain, as well as reduce the risk of cancers.

High levels of magnesium in beetroot help keep bones healthy and able to absorb calcium.

BUYING AND STORING GUIDE

Get two for the price of one when buying both the root and the greens. Look for firm, smooth, deep-red or yellow bulbs with fresh, bright greens attached.

If buying fresh beetroot from the market, twist rather than cut off the greens before storing the beetroot in the fridge. Keeping some of the stem attached prevents the beetroot from bleeding.

Cooked beetroot can be frozen, canned or pickled.

GREEN FINGERS

Beetroot is in the same family as spinach and is loosely related to Swiss chard.

Beetroot has natural red pigment which stains everything. Salt and lemon juice are effective in removing stains from your hands.

It is preferable to grow beetroot in cooler climates since hot climates cause the roots to be quite tough.

Beetroot is a good choice for containers as long as the soil has good drainage and it is kept well watered. Harvesting occurs within 40 days of planting if the correct growing environment is respected.

Beetroot tart with baby rocket

SERVES 1

This is such a simple tart and yet always creates a wow from my guests because it is so beautiful on a plate. If beetroot is not your favourite, use grilled tomatoes and basil.

▶ Preheat the oven to 200°C (400°F).

▶ Lightly dust a work surface with flour then roll out the puff pastry until it is 4 mm (¼ in) thick.

▶ Cut out 4 discs with a 11.5 cm (4½ in) round pastry cutter. Using a sharp knife, lightly score around the pastry discs 1 cm (½ in) away from the edge, trying not to cut through the pastry.

▶ Brush the edges with the beaten egg and place the pasty discs onto a nonstick baking sheet. Poke a few holes in the pastry and place in the oven on the middle shelf.

▶ Bake for 20 minutes, or until golden. Once cooked, remove from the oven and leave to cool.

1 sheet ready-made puff pastry, thawed

1 egg, beaten

Topping

1 cup cream cheese

½ cup heavy cream

juice of 1 lemon

4 large cooked beetroot (master recipe, see p. 105), thinly sliced and patted dry

Salad

¼ cup olive oil

½ tablespoon lemon juice

salt and pepper

2 cups baby rocket

¼ cup Parmesan shavings

Topping

▶ Blend the cream cheese, cream and lemon juice together. Spread over the base of the cooled tart shells.

▶ Arrange the beetroot slices on top of the cheese mixture. Be sure that beetroot slices are relatively dry so that the pink juice does not run onto the white cream.

Salad

▶ Whisk the olive oil and lemon juice together in a small bowl. Season with salt and pepper. Pour the vinaigrette over the baby rocket and toss.

▶ To serve, place individual tarts on plates and top with rocket and Parmesan shavings.

Use leftover puff pastry to make cheese straws. Roll out pastry, sprinkle with cheese, fold over pastry and flatten with a rolling pin. Cut the pastry into strips, twist them and place on a baking sheet lined with parchment paper. Bake at 180°C (350°F) for 10 minutes, or until golden.

Quinoa salad with beetroot, oranges and spinach

· **SERVES 6**

Using red quinoa in this salad reduces the possibility of creating a pink salad. I also only toss in the beetroot at the end so that they create as little pink effect as possible.

2 cups cooked red quinoa

4 roasted beetroot (master recipe, see p. 105)

2 oranges, segmented and juice reserved (master recipe, see p. 185)

1½ cups baby spinach

¼ cup sunflower seeds, toasted

½ cup goat's cheese

Orange dressing

1 teaspoon Dijon mustard

¼ cup orange juice

1 tablespoon white balsamic vinegar

¼ cup good-quality olive oil

1 tablespoon chopped fresh flat-leaf parsley

Sea salt and pepper

▸ Cook the quinoa in boiling water following package directions.

▸ Cut the beetroot and orange segments into bite-sized pieces.

▸ Whisk the mustard, orange juice and vinegar together in a small bowl. Slowly add olive oil to create an emulsion. Stir in the parsley and season with salt and pepper.

▸ To assemble the salad, place the cooked quinoa into a large bowl. Toss with spinach and the orange segments. Carefully fold in the dressing. Add the beetroot but do not stir too much otherwise the salad will turn pink.

▸ Top with sunflower seeds and a crumbling of soft goat's cheese.

You can use rocket instead of spinach to give a bigger flavor boost.

Tomato and beetroot soup

SERVES 8 AS SHOOTERS FOR AN APPETIZER

*Be careful when blending
hot liquids because they
expand and cause kitchen
catastrophes. Only fill the jug
half full if the liquid is hot.*

*I love to serve shooters of soup as appetizers. I bought some lovely glass tea cups in
Morocco and they always create a stir. Look around your house and see what can be used.*

2 tablespoons olive oil

½ cup finely chopped onion

2 cloves garlic, minced

1 tablespoon cumin seeds

3 cups baked beetroot
(master recipe, see p. 105), chopped

1 cup cherry tomatoes,
roasted (see p. 119)

2 cups chicken or vegetable stock

Sea salt and freshly
ground black pepper

▸ Heat 1 tablespoon olive oil in a pan and sweat the onion for a few minutes
until soft. Add the garlic and cumin and continue cooking for a few
minutes over medium heat.

▸ Stir in the beetroot, roasted tomatoes and stock, turn up the heat and
bring to a boil. Simmer for 10 minutes.

▸ Remove from the heat and allow the soup to cool.

▸ Transfer the soup to a blender and process until completely smooth. Taste
and adjust the seasoning if necessary.

▸ Add more stock if soup is too thick.

▸ Pour the heated soup into shooter glasses and serve immediately.

Potato latkes with beetroot cream

MAKES 32 MINI POTATO LATKES

A different way to cook boring old potatoes. The beetroot cream makes them special enough to be served as an hors d'oeuvre.

Beetroot cream

½ cup baked beetroot (approx.2) (master recipe, see p. 105), cut into pieces

½ cup Greek yoghurt

2 tablespoons (½ log) soft goat's cheese

½ tablespoon lemon juice

handful of fresh parsley

1 teaspoon dried marjoram

Salt and pepper to taste

Potato latkes

2 cups peeled and grated potatoes

1 tablespoon grated onion

1 egg, beaten

3 tablespoons flour

1½ teaspoons salt

2½ tablespoons grapeseed oil, for frying

Beetroot cream

▸ Blend the beetroot, yoghurt and goat's cheese in a food processor until smooth.

▸ Add lemon, parsley, marjoram and salt and pepper and process until fully blended.

Potato latkes

▸ Place the grated potatoes in a tea towel and squeeze out as much moisture as possible.

▸ Mix the potatoes, onion, egg, flour and salt together in a medium bowl.

▸ Heat the oil in a large skillet, then drop heaped tablespoons of the potato mixture into the oil. Press with the back of a spoon to create flattened patties.

▸ Once browned on one side, flip over and cook the other side. Remove from the skillet and drain on paper towel. Keep warm in the oven while you make the rest.

▸ Serve individual latkes with beetroot cream and a sprig of marjoram.

Make mini latkes to serve as appetizers. Leftover boiled potatoes can also be used, though they do not have the same grated consistency.

Beetroot greens are wonderful rinsed, cut up into pieces and sautéed in olive oil with garlic.

Red bell pepper

This is my youngest son Frédéric's favourite vegetable, raw or cooked. It is one that I often have in my refrigerator to whip up into a hummus or a side for grilled meat. It is also one of the few vegetables that can be grilled and kept for a while in the fridge topped with a little olive oil.

Master recipe

Roasted red bell peppers

MAKES APPROXIMATELY 1½ - 2 CUPS

4 whole red bell peppers	▸ Preheat the oven grill (broiler).
½ cup olive oil	▸ Place the bell peppers on a baking sheet in the middle of the oven and grill until the skin is blistered on all sides.
1 clove garlic, peeled and sliced into slivers	▸ Place the bell peppers in a bowl, cover and set aside for about 10 minutes. This will allow the skin to separate from the flesh of the bell peppers. Carefully peel off the skin.
	▸ Cut the bell peppers in half, remove the seeds and the stem and place in a shallow bottomed dish. Cover with olive oil and slices of garlic.

HEALTH BENEFITS

Red bell peppers are bursting with anti-oxidants and vitamins A and C, making them a superfood.

The vitamin C in red bell peppers helps in boosting the immune system, slowing the aging process, and aids in the absorption of iron.

Vitamin A is responsible for enhancing night vision.

The combination of vitamin B6 and magnesium in a bell pepper is effective in reducing premenstrual symptoms, as well as hypertension and bloating.

The lycopene in red bell peppers is what makes the vegetable red and is responsible for the increased prevention of many cancers.

BUYING AND STORING GUIDE

Red bell peppers are a mature (fully ripened) version of a green bell pepper, while yellow and orange bell peppers are different varieties.

When buying bell peppers, search for fruits that are firm, vivid in colour and heavy for their size.

Bell peppers are best stored in the fridge, but be sure that they are dry otherwise they will rot.

For those with a cellar, bell peppers can be stored there for up to 3 months.

Bell peppers can be frozen whole without being blanched. They may also be roasted and kept in jars with an oil dressing and added garlic and fresh herbs.

GREEN FINGERS

All peppers can be grown in gardens and containers, but they need a lot of sun and should be well staked before they start to grow so that you do not disturb the root system.

Pick as often as possible to increase pepper production.

When grilling bell peppers, be sure to keep the seeds, stems and skins for the compost or worms.

Grilled chicken breasts with red bell pepper cream

SERVES 4

Serving this red bell pepper sauce with grilled chicken jazzes up the dish without too much effort. I also use this sauce on grilled fish.

2 tablespoons olive oil

1 clove garlic, minced

1 teaspoon chilli powder

1 teaspoon dried oregano

4 chicken breast fillets, pounded

Red bell pepper cream

2 tablespoons olive oil (can use oil from master recipe)

2 roasted red bell peppers (master recipe, see p. 113)

½ red chilli pepper, seeded and sliced

1 tablespoon minced garlic

2 tablespoons apple cider vinegar

juice of ½ medium lemon

½ cup whipping cream

Salt and freshly ground black pepper

Sauce can be made ahead and kept in the fridge for 3 days This is also a great sauce for pasta.

▶ Mix the oil, garlic, chilli powder and oregano together in a small bowl. Add the chicken and coat with the mixture. Set aside for at least 30 minutes.

▶ While the chicken is marinating, make the red pepper cream. Heat 2 tablespoons of the olive oil in a pan over medium heat. Add the bell peppers, chilli and garlic and sauté for 2–3 minutes until the vegetables are tender.

▶ Add the vinegar, lemon juice and cream and cook for an additional 2–3 minutes. Remove from the heat and allow to cool to room temperature.

▶ Purée the pepper mixture in a food processor or blender and season with salt and pepper. Return the pepper mixture to the pan and reheat before serving.

▶ Heat the grill and cook the chicken fillets over medium heat for approximately 5 minutes per side.

▶ Serve with the sauce.

Roasted red bell pepper, caper and buffalo mozzarella bruschetta

MAKES 8 PIECES

This easy bruschetta uses up old bread while also celebrating the flavours of summer. I often add some tomato if I do not have enough roasted red bell peppers.

2 diced roasted red bell peppers (master recipe, see p. 113)

½ large buffalo mozzarella ball, cut into mini cubes

1 tablespoon drained capers, chopped

2 tablespoons chopped fresh basil

2 tablespoons olive oil

¼ teaspoon salt

¼ teaspoon freshly ground black pepper

½ baguette, sliced into 8 pieces

1 clove garlic, halved

1 tablespoon balsamic vinegar

▶ Preheat the oven grill (broiler).

▶ Combine the peppers, mozzarella, capers, basil and 1 teaspoon of oil in a medium bowl. Season with salt and pepper.

▶ Rub both sides of the baguette with the cut sides of the garlic.

▶ Arrange the bread slices in a single layer on a baking sheet. Brush one side with the remaining olive oil and toast under the grill. Be sure not to let burn.

▶ Top the untoasted side of the bread with the pepper mixture. Drizzle with the balsamic vinegar and serve.

When making any bruschetta be sure that all the ingredients in the bruschetta mixture are of similar size.

Day-old baguette works best for making any sort of bruschetta and is a good way of using up leftover baguette or any other bread.

Roasted Mediterranean lentil salad

SERVES 6

This simple salad is a quick and easy one to prepare. It is full of goodness, using lentils, vegetables and seeds. Use this recipe as a guide and add ingredients as you like.

¾ cup dried green lentils (you want to end up with 2 cups cooked)

2 cups water

1 roasted red bell pepper (master recipe, see p. 113), thinly sliced

½ red onion, thinly sliced

¼ cup Kalamata olives, pitted

2 tablespoons chopped fresh basil

1 tablespoon chopped fresh parsley

1½ cups chopped rocket

¼ cup sunflower seeds, toasted

Vinaigrette

3 tablespoons balsamic vinegar

1 tablespoon lemon juice

⅓ cup extra virgin olive oil

½ teaspoon honey

Sea salt and black pepper to taste

▸ Boil the lentils in the water until soft but not mushy. Drain and place in a medium-sized bowl.

▸ While the lentils are cooking, prepare the vinaigrette by mixing all the ingredients together to create an emulsion. Set aside.

▸ Add the red bell pepper, onion, olives, basil, parsley and rocket to the lentils and toss gently.

▸ Mix the vinaigrette into the salad and set aside for 20 minutes before serving to allow the flavours to blend. Add salt and pepper to taste.

▸ Top with sunflower seeds just before serving.

This salad is also good with cheese, such as shavings of Parmesan or grated asiago cheese.

To decrease the cooking time of lentils or any dried beans, soak them for a few hours or overnight. Rinse with clean water and then boil until cooked. The cooking time will be reduced by half.

Tomato

The abundance of red tomatoes is often greeted with great excitement, followed by a feeling of sadness. Summer has created her little treasures but autumn is soon to follow.

Master recipe

Roasted tomatoes

MAKES APPROXIMATELY 1 CUP

2 cups red grape or cherry tomatoes OR 8 tomatoes, halved

4 cloves garlic, halved

2 tablespoons extra-virgin olive oil

Sea salt

▶ Preheat the oven to 200°C (400°F).

▶ Mix the tomatoes with the olive oil, garlic and sea salt in a roasting pan.

▶ If using large tomatoes, slice them thickly (or in half, if not too large), drizzle with olive oil, sprinkle with pieces of garlic and sea salt.

▶ Roast in the middle of the oven for 15–20 minutes until the tomatoes are beginning to shrivel and explode.

▶ If using large tomatoes, roast until the halves begin to shrivel and brown on the sides.

▶ Blend for a pizza or pasta sauce or use whole as a topping for grilled fish or chicken.

HEALTH BENEFITS

Tomatoes contain an anti-oxidant called lycopene, which is responsible for the redness of the fruit as well as the properties needed to protect against certain cancers.

The greater the heat, the more effective the lycopene, so cooked tomatoes are even better than raw ones.

The combination of folate, potassium, iron and vitamin B in tomatoes helps in reducing the risk of heart disease.

The beta-carotene and vitamins A and C in tomatoes help in boosting the immune system as well as warding off age-related vision and skin problems.

BUYING AND STORING GUIDE

Buy deep coloured, firm tomatoes with a slightly sweet aroma. Make sure that the smaller cherry tomatoes do not have wrinkles; like humans, it is a sign of age.

When testing the firmness of a tomato, use your palm rather than your fingers to apply pressure to prevent damaging the fruit.

Tomatoes are best stored at room temperature and never in a plastic bag.

Tomatoes can be frozen fresh (without skins) or cooked. They can also be canned if there is lack of freezer space. Remember to keep the seeds since they contain significant levels of nutrients.

The acidity of tomatoes can affect the resin lining of tin cans, causing the leaching of Bisphenol A (BPA), a chemical used to make plastics. This can lead to reproductive problems, heart disease and diabetes. It is best to buy bottled rather than canned tomatoes.

GREEN FINGERS

All parts of the tomato plant are toxic except for the fruit so keep those pots of tomatoes away from children and pets.

The leaves and stems of the tomato plant contain a compound called glycoalkaloid, which can cause extreme nervousness and stomach upsets.

Tomatoes continue to ripen off the vine.

Cherry tomatoes are ideal for container gardening, including pots and hanging baskets, but remember to give tomatoes something to climb since they are vines. If hanging, give them something to attach to.

Seedlings need lots of sunlight and well watered roots.

Tomato and fennel soup with cheese croutons

SERVES 4

The roasted vegetables give a greater depth of flavour to the soup. The dash of Pernod helps to enhance the fennel bulb.

Keep fennel ends and other vegetable offcuts in a bag in the fridge (few days) or frozen in the freezer (few weeks) to make an easy vegetable stock.

2 cups roasted tomatoes (master recipe, see p. 119) (or roast tomatoes with the rest of the vegetables)

1 fennel bulb, chopped

2 orange, yellow or red bell peppers, cut into bite-sized pieces

1 onion, cut into bite-sized pieces

3 cloves garlic, unpeeled

2 tablespoons olive oil

Sea salt

1 tablespoon cumin seeds

1 tablespoon aniseed

3 cups vegetable or chicken stock

1 tablespoon Pernod

¼ cup cream

Cheese croutons

1 cup cubes of crusty bread

2 tablespoons olive oil

1 tablespoon finely grated Parmesan cheese

Sea salt

▸ Preheat the oven to 180°C (350°F).

▸ Mix all the vegetables together on a baking sheet and toss with olive oil and sea salt.

▸ Roast for 40–50 minutes until the vegetables are fork tender and browned.

▸ Transfer the roasted vegetables to a large saucepan, add the cumin, aniseed and stock. Bring to a boil and cook for 20 minutes.

▸ Allow the soup to cool before blending. Once blended, add the Pernod.

▸ Reheat and serve with a swirl of cream and cheese croutons (see below).

Cheese croutons

▸ Toss the cubes of bread with the olive oil, grated Parmesan cheese and sea salt.

▸ Place on a baking sheet and bake at 180°C (350°F) for 20 minutes. Toss the croutons halfway through the cooking time.

Couscous with roasted tomatoes, yellow bell peppers, olives and fresh herbs

SERVES 6

This is a quick dish that requires very little skill but offers tons of flavour. Most of the ingredients can be grown in your garden or on your balcony in boxes. Add a red chilli pepper to give a little kick.

2 cups cooked couscous (cook according to package instructions)

¼ cup brine-cured black olives, pitted

½ cup chopped roasted tomatoes (master recipe, see p. 119)

½ cup bite-sized pieces yellow bell pepper

Salt and pepper

¼ cup fruity olive oil

2 tablespoons lemon juice

2 tablespoons chopped fresh flat-leaf parsley

2 tablespoons chopped fresh mint

¼ cup chopped baby rocket

▸ Place the cooked couscous into a medium-sized bowl and stir in the olives, roasted tomatoes and yellow bell pepper. Season to taste.

▸ Mix the oil, lemon juice and fresh herbs together in a small bowl. Pour over the couscous and combine well.

▸ Serve with grilled meat.

If you have fresh herbs that are on their last legs, cut them up and mix them into ½ cup of softened salted butter with a minced clove of garlic and a shallot. Roll into a log and wrap in waxed paper and freeze. Use sliced on grilled meats or vegetables to give extra flavour.

Garlic prawns and roasted tomato pasta

SERVES 4

When buying prawns, look for farm-raised rather than ocean caught, since no by-catch is produced.

Reserve prawn shells and heads and keep frozen in the freezer to make a stock by simmering the shells with yellow onion, garlic, water and a touch of white wine. Very tasty.

Olive oil, for frying

2 shallots, minced

1 tablespoon minced garlic

1 small red chilli pepper, seeded and chopped

20 medium prawns, shelled and deveined, tail on

¼ cup lemon juice

¼ cup white wine

1 cup roasted tomatoes (master recipe, see p. 119)

1 jar roasted artichoke hearts, chopped

16 oz (450 g) uncooked linguini

¼ cup chopped fresh basil

Sea salt and pepper

▶ Heat a little olive oil in a medium skillet. Sauté the shallots until softened, then add the garlic and chilli pepper.

▶ Once the garlic has softened, add the prawns and sauté. When the prawns turn slightly pink, deglaze the pan with lemon juice and white wine. Reduce the liquid by half before adding the roasted tomatoes and artichoke hearts. Cook for an additional minute before taking off the heat.

▶ Bring a large saucepan of salted water to a boil then add the pasta. Once *al dente*, reserve a cup of pasta water and drain the pasta.

▶ Return the pasta to the saucepan and add the tomato and prawn mixture. If too dry, add some of the reserved pasta water.

▶ Mix in the fresh basil, season with salt and pepper and serve.

If basil leaves (or any fresh green herb) are beginning to turn, chop roughly and place into individual ice cube trays with a little water. Freeze for future use.

Baked white fish with tomatoes, caperberries and basil ragout

SERVES 4

I have been making this dish for years since it is an easy, no fuss, one skillet recipe. It has a brilliant color, demands very little work yet offers great taste.

Ingredients	Method
2 tablespoons flour	▶ Preheat the oven to 160°C (325°F).
Salt and pepper	▶ Place the flour with a little salt and pepper in a large, wide bowl.
4 white fish fillets	▶ Dredge the fish fillets through the flour so that they are lightly coated.
2 tablespoons olive oil	▶ Heat the oil in a skillet and fry the fish fillets until lightly coloured. Place the fillets in a baking dish and set aside.
½ cup white wine	
½ cup fish or chicken stock	▶ Pour the wine into the skillet and bring to a boil. Scrape up any bits that are left on the bottom of the pan. Once the wine is reduced by half, add the stock and continue cooking. Add the tomatoes and caperberries to the simmering stock, stir and cook briefly.
1 cup roasted tomatoes (master recipe, see p. 119)	
8 caperberries	▶ Remove from the heat and pour the sauce over the fish. Bake in the oven for 5-10 minutes then add the basil and serve.
1 bunch fresh basil, sliced thinly	▶ This fish dish can be prepared until the last step so it is great with guests.

Stock made from reserved prawn shells can also be used to make the sauce.

Apple

*The u-pick-it season for apples
was one that was always relished
in our family. The crunch of a
freshly picked Macintosh apple
and the excitement of having a hot
mulled cider after an afternoon
of work in the orchard was all
part of the weekend experience.*

Master recipe

Apple sauce

MAKES 4 CUPS

1.5 kg (3 lb) apples, peeled, cored and chopped (no need to peel, if organic)

½ teaspoon ground cinnamon

1 tablespoon brown sugar, honey or maple syrup (if apples are sweet then you'll need less)

½ cup water

▸ Place the apples in a large saucepan.

▸ Add cinnamon, sugar and water. Cover and bring to a boil. Allow the mixture to simmer until the apples are completely softened, approximately 15 minutes.

▸ Remove from the heat and cool before passing through a food mill.

▸ If the apples are peeled, place the cooked apples in a food processor and whizz until it reaches the desired consistency. I like slightly lumpy apple sauce so I am careful not to process too much.

HEALTH BENEFITS

Zero fat and cholesterol with fibre make a red apple the perfect fat-burning snack food, while keeping heart disease at bay.

The anti-oxidants in apples are believed to help reduce the risk of various cancers, including breast, colon and liver cancers.

The high levels of the flavonoids, quercetin and naringin, in apples are believed to be responsible for lowering the risk of lung cancer and increasing bone density in menopausal women.

BUYING AND STORING GUIDE

Choose apples that are firm, sweet-smelling and have a slightly yellow-green background beyond the apparent red part. The colour is obviously dependent on the type.

Keep apples stored in a cool dark place, such as the fridge, since they ripen at least twice as fast at room temperature.

Buy organic apples since this fruit absorbs high levels of pesticides and apple trees are often over-sprayed to keep disease away.

Keep apples away from potatoes since aging spuds give off gases that cause apples to spoil.

Be sure that no rotten apples are in the mix since a rotten apple will cause all the rest to spoil. That might also be considered a life lesson!

GREEN FINGERS

There are over 7,500 varieties of apples worldwide and all of these varieties have trees that take up to five years of growth to produce their first edible apple.

An apple is made up of 80–85% water.

Certain apple tree varieties can be planted in pots, but remember to add chives since they are a natural deterrent to the apple scab.

Worms, chickens and pigs love apple cores.

Did you know that apple skins boiled in water make an effective cleaning agent for aluminum pots and pans?

Apple sauce spice muffins

MAKES 12 LARGE MUFFINS

I love apple crumble so this apple muffin recipe is influenced by my need to have a bit of c
crumble with my muffin.

1½ cups flour

1½ teaspoons baking power

½ teaspoon bicarbonate of soda

½ teaspoon ground cinnamon

½ teaspoon ground ginger

¼ teaspoon freshly grated nutmeg

¼ teaspoon salt

2 eggs

½ cup packed light brown sugar

½ cup butter, melted

⅓ cup buttermilk

1 cup apple sauce
(master recipe, see p. 127)

⅔ cup peeled and
chopped red apple

Topping

2 tablespoons butter

2 tablespoon oats

½ teaspoon ground cinnamon

½ teaspoon ground ginger

2 tablespoons flour

3 tablespoons brown sugar

▸ Preheat the oven to 200°C (400°F). Grease 12 muffin cups.

▸ Sift the flour, baking powder, bicarbonate of soda, cinnamon, ginger, nutmeg and salt together in a large bowl.

▸ In a separate bowl, whisk the eggs and brown sugar together until well combined.

▸ Whisk the melted butter into the egg mixture, a little at a time, until creamy. Mix in the buttermilk, then stir in apple sauce and apple pieces.

▸ Fold the flour mixture into the egg mixture, making sure not to over mix. Divide the batter among the muffin cups.

▸ Stir all the topping ingredients together and sprinkle on top of the batter. Bake until the muffins are puffed and golden, about 20 minutes.

▸ Cool in the muffin pan on a rack 5 minutes, then remove the muffins from the pan.

If you do not have buttermilk, add 1 teaspoon of white vinegar to one cup of whole milk. Set aside for 5–10 minutes to let it curdle and presto! Buttermilk.

Apple-stuffed pork chops

SERVES 4

This is a great make-ahead meal that is tasty and easy to prepare. The fennel complements both pork and apple beautifully.

4 boneless pork chops, 4 cm (1½ in) thick

Salt and pepper to taste

¼ cup apple juice

¼ cup apple cider vinegar

½ teaspoon dried sage

¼ teaspoon crushed fennel seeds

Oil, for frying

2 tablespoons minced fennel bulb (½ small bulb)

2 cloves garlic, minced

1 tablespoon Pernod (aniseed-flavoured liqueur)

⅔ cup apple sauce (master recipe, see p. 127)

¼ cup apple cider

Fennel is sometimes difficult to cut so the best method is to remove the V-shaped core. Once removed, cut the bulb in half and then slice each side thinly.

▶ Lay the pork chops flat on a work surface and cut a horizontal slit through the thickest portion of each chop to form a pocket. Place the chops in a medium baking dish. Season with salt and pepper.

▶ Mix the apple juice, vinegar, sage and fennel seed together and pour over the chops. Set aside for 1 hour, turning the chops halfway through.

▶ Preheat the oven to 180°C (350°F).

▶ Remove the chops from the marinade and set aside.

▶ Heat a little oil in a frying pan and sauté the fennel and garlic together for 1 minute. Once softened, add the Pernod then the apple sauce. Stir and remove from the heat. Season with salt and pepper

▶ Once cool, divide the apple sauce mixture into four and stuff into each pork pocket.

▶ Brush oil onto a griddle pan, heat up and add the chops; be careful not to let the stuffing slip out.

▶ Cook the chops for 3–4 minutes on each side, or until lines are well marked on the meat.

▶ Transfer to a baking dish and pour the apple cider over the pork chops. Add any additional stuffing that might have fallen out. Bake for 35 minutes.

Apple sauce oat squares

MAKES 12–16

These squares are easy to make and are so moist that they melt in your mouth. They are also not too sweet, which can be dangerous since it is easy to eat the entire batch.

½ cup + 1 tablespoon
unsalted butter, softened

¾ cup packed brown sugar

1¾ cups flour

½ teaspoon sea salt

½ teaspoon bicarbonate of soda

1 cup rolled oats

1 cup apple sauce
(master recipe, see p. 127)

½ cup roasted pecans,
chopped roughly

▸ Preheat the oven to 180°C (350°F). Grease a square baking pan.

▸ Cream the butter and brown sugar together in a large mixing bowl.

▸ Sift the flour, salt and bicarbonate of soda together and add to the butter mixture.

▸ Add the oats and mix well. Using your fingers is most effective and satisfying to achieve the best consistency.

▸ Divide the crumbly dough into two-thirds and one-third.

▸ Press the larger amount of dough into the prepared pan.

▸ Spread the apple sauce over the dough.

▸ Add the pecans to the remaining crumbly dough and sprinkle over the apple sauce. It will look a bit like a crumble topping.

▸ Bake for 30 minutes. Cool in the pan and then cut into squares.

1

2

3

4

Poori stuffed with apple sauce

SERVES 6

After my trip to India, I realized that it was so simple to whip up some yeastless bread. I loved these simple pooris so I came up with the idea of turning them into sweet rather than savoury treats.

1½ cups all-purpose flour
or wholewheat flour

1 teaspoon salt

1½ tablespoons coconut oil, melted

1 teaspoon ground cinnamon

½ cup water plus an additional
2 tablespoons if needed

1 cup apple sauce
(master recipe, see p. 127)

1 cup vegetable oil

1 teaspoon ground cinnamon
mixed with 1 tablespoon sugar

▸ Mix the flour with the cinnamon, salt and coconut oil. Add a little of the water and start kneading. Add more water if necessary. The dough should be slightly sticky and elastic in feel.

▸ Divide the dough into 16 equal tiny balls. Using a rolling pin, roll individual balls into a 7.5 cm (3 in) diameter circle.

▸ Place 1 teaspoon of apple sauce in the centre of each pastry round and fold over to create a half-moon. To seal, use a fork to lightly push down around the edges.

▸ Heat the oil in a deep pan or wok. To test if the oil is at the right temperature, drop a tiny piece of dough in the oil and if it rises up immediately, it is ready to fry the pooris.

▸ Drop one poori at a time into the hot oil and allow to cook for about 30 seconds on each side. They should turn golden brown.

▸ Remove from the oil using a slotted spoon and drain on paper towels. Sprinkle with a mixture of sugar and cinnamon or icing sugar.

▸ Serve immediately with tea or coffee.

Strawberry

When my son Patrick was born, it was summer and strawberry season was in full swing. Days before I gave birth, we went out to pick strawberries. I remember my determination to use up the thousands of berries that we picked before he arrived. I have never made so much jam in my life!

Master recipe

Balsamic strawberries

MAKES 2 CUPS

2 cups hulled and cut strawberries

1 tablespoon balsamic vinegar

1 tablespoon icing sugar

▸ Place the strawberries into a bowl.

▸ Sprinkle with balsamic vinegar and sugar. Toss to coat and set aside for 30 minutes.

BUYING AND STORING GUIDE

HEALTH BENEFITS

Strawberries are full of vitamin C, helping to boost the immune system, keeping skin looking young and eyes free of cataracts.

The flavonoids in strawberries are good for a healthy heart and joints as they reduce bad cholesterol and have important anti-inflammatory properties.

Strawberries contain fibre, which aids digestion.

When buying strawberries, look for bright red berries with their green caps intact.

Once picked, strawberries no longer ripen so do not buy green or yellow berries.

Never wash strawberries until you are ready to eat them since they act as sponges. Once they are full of water, they begin to deteriorate.

Store strawberries on paper towel in a sealed container in the fridge for a few days.

Remove any damaged strawberries since mould grows quickly on these berries.

Whole or cut, washed and hulled berries can be frozen on a tray and then placed in an airtight container in the freezer.

GREEN FINGERS

Strawberries can be grown in containers. Ripe berries appear within 30 days of planting. Great for balconies.

The growing season for strawberries is late spring through early autumn.

Strawberries like well drained, well watered soil with at least 6 hours of sunlight.

Strawberry juice combined with honey will reduce inflammation or sunburn. Rub the mixture thoroughly into the skin before rinsing off with warm water and lemon juice.

Breakfast delight

SERVES 4

This breakfast in a glass is reminiscent of my days in bush camps. We would often prepare fruit, yoghurt and granola cups to take out on game drives for the clients who get up at 5:30 a.m. to see the animals.

1 cup strawberries (master recipe p. 135) or hulled and sliced

1–1½ cups Greek yoghurt

¼ cup honey

1–1½ cups homemade granola (see below)

Homemade granola

½ cup coconut oil

¼ cup honey or maple syrup

1 cup raw wheat germ

3 cups old-fashioned oats

1 cup raw almonds, chopped

½ cup pecans, chopped

⅓ cup dried cranberries and blueberries

¾ cup puffed rice

Granola

▸ Preheat the oven to 180°C (350°F).

▸ Stir the oil, honey and wheat germ together in a large bowl, then stir in the oats and nuts.

▸ Bake for 15 minutes, then stir and continue to bake, checking and stirring every few minutes, until golden brown, about 30 minutes in all.

▸ Stir in the dried fruit and puffed rice and then let cool to room temperature. Store in a sealed container for up to 2 weeks.

To serve

▸ Be creative with your presentation. Either layer the fruit, granola and yoghurt, and then drizzle with honey, or set out bowls of cut strawberries and yoghurt with a drizzle of honey and granola. Enjoy!

Making your own granola ensures that you know exactly how much sugar is being added.

Strawberry tiramisu

SERVES 6–8

Tiramisu is my boys' favourite dessert. Last year, when I had an excess of overripe strawberries in my fridge, I created this variation of a tiramisu. It was very well received.

4 cups strawberries, sliced, or a mix of leftover balsamic strawberries (master recipe, see p. 135) and fresh ones

5 tablespoons sugar

3 eggs, separated

1 cup mascarpone cheese

1 cup whipping cream

1 cup orange juice combined with strawberry juice from berries

1 tablespoon strawberry liqueur

1 large package of ladyfingers

100 g (4 oz) dark chocolate, grated

▸ Place the strawberries in a bowl and sprinkle with 2 tablespoons of sugar. If using balsamic strawberries, this step can be skipped. Set aside for at least 4 hours or overnight to macerate (produce juices to be used for dipping the ladyfingers).

▸ Beat the egg yolks and remaining 3 tablespoons sugar in the top of a double boiler until the mixture becomes pale yellow and thicker in consistency, 3–4 minutes.

▸ Remove from the heat and add the mascarpone cheese. Beat with a hand-held electric mixer until smooth and creamy, 2–3 minutes.

▸ Beat the whipping cream until stiff peaks are formed. In another bowl, beat egg whites with 1 tablespoon of sugar until stiff peaks are formed.

▸ Fold the cream into the whipped egg whites then fold the mixture into the marscapone mixture.

▸ Strain the juice from the berries (½ cup or so) and add ½ cup of orange juice and 1 tablespoon strawberry liqueur (optional).

▸ Submerge each ladyfinger in the juice mixture and then place on the bottom of a glass or ceramic serving dish (about 2 in/5 cm deep). If there is not enough juice, use more orange juice.

▸ To create the layers, begin with a layer of ladyfingers, followed by a layer of berries and then a layer of the mascarpone mixture.

▸ Arrange a second layer of soaked ladyfingers over the mascarpone cream, then spread the remaining mascarpone cream evenly over the top. One layer may be sufficient depending on the size of the dish.

▸ Dust the tiramisu with grated chocolate.

▸ Refrigerate for at least 4 hours or up to 1 day before serving.

Strawberry vodka lemonade

MAKES ENOUGH FOR THE SUMMER OR ONE WILD PARTY

This is a simple one-step recipe that works well with plain as well as balsamic strawberries. It also looks great in a glass bottle with a spigot for easy access.

1 cup balsamic strawberries (master recipe, see p. 135)

12 fresh mint leaves

1 teaspoon lemon juice (if using fresh strawberries)

1 bottle of vodka (1.75L)

▸ Place the strawberries, mint leaves and lemon juice in a sealable container.

▸ Pour vodka over the fruit mixture and seal the container. Set aside for a week.

▸ The strawberries will turn white as the vodka turns red. The vodka can last for months without ever removing the ghostly pale fruit or straining the liquid.

Serving suggestion:

The vodka has a lovely berry flavour that can be enjoyed on its own as a shot or can be made into the following cocktail:

2 parts vodka

1 part lemonade

1 part soda water

▸ Serve in a highball with a slice of lime, a mint leaf and a fresh strawberry for colour.

Quick strawberry jam

SERVES 6–8

This is so easy and a great way to use up a strawberry salad from the previous day or strawberries that are losing their lustre.

1 cup balsamic strawberries (master recipe, see p. 135)

¼ cup white sugar

1 teaspoon lemon juice

▸ Place the berries and sugar in a small saucepan over medium heat. Cook, stirring constantly, so that the sugar does not burn.

▸ Once the fruit has softened, about 5 minutes, add the lemon juice. Continue cooking until the strawberries have lost their shape.

▸ Can be served warm as a fruit compote with pancakes or cold as a jam with scones or toast.

Watermelon

Sweet, succulent watermelon juice dripping down the sides of our cheeks was a norm when I was growing up. It is mind boggling to see how watermelon has evolved over the years into a raw and grilled delicacy.

Master recipe

Watermelon with mint

SERVINGS DEPENDS ON SIZE OF WATERMELON

½ watermelon

¼ cup mint simple syrup (see p. 69)

fresh mint leaves, for garnishing

▸ Cut the watermelon into slices and then remove the rind. Cut each slice into three pieces. Place on a platter.

▸ Drizzle lightly with minted sugar syrup. Garnish with mint leaves and serve.

HEALTH BENEFITS

Watermelon is high in anti-oxidants, including vitamin C, which is a great immune booster. It also contains vitamin A, which is effective in eye health and vitamin B6, which is helpful with brain function.

Rich in potassium and magnesium, the nutrients in watermelon help to control blood pressure and in turn prevent strokes and kidney disorders.

Watermelon continue to ripen and build up anti-oxidants after they are picked. Chilling stops this process so refrain from storing watermelon in the fridge.

Watermelon rind has less sugar than the flesh and is rich in anti-oxidants.

Athletes use the entire fruit, rind, flesh and seeds when making juice.

BUYING AND STORING GUIDE

When buying watermelon, look for green ones with few white marks and a yellow area on one side. This yellow patch proves that the melon was on the ground when ripening.

If buying a piece of the whole watermelon, make sure that the seeds are dark.

Watermelons are primarily grown during the heat of the summer season, the perfect sweet and juicy treat.

If the watermelon sounds hollow when it is slapped, it is ripe and ready to be eaten.

Watermelon can be stored at room temperature, not overly hot, for up to 10 days. It is best to cool prior to eating.

Watermelon can be cut into pieces, frozen on a tray and then placed in an airtight container in the freezer for up to a year. The consistency does change though.

GREEN FINGERS

Most watermelons found in your neighborhood store or market are produced locally and therefore have a minute carbon footprint.

Watermelon seeds can be toasted in the oven, spiced and eaten as a healthy snack.

Chickens, horses and pigs love watermelon rind if it is not being used in the kitchen for making jam.

Watermelon and lemon spritzer

SERVES 4

What to do with all that extra watermelon taking up too much space in the fridge?
Reduce it in a purée and use for a refreshing afternoon drink.

4 cups watermelon pieces
(master recipe, see p. 143)

¼ cup lemon juice

10 fresh mint leaves

1 cup ginger ale

sprigs of fresh mint and extra pieces
of watermelon, for garnishing

▸ Purée the watermelon pieces in a
  blender. Add the lemon juice and
  mint and whizz until well blended.

▸ Half-fill highball glasses with the
  watermelon purée. Add some ice
  cubes and top off with ginger ale.

▸ Garnish with a sprig of mint and a
  piece of watermelon.

Watermelon granita

SERVES 6

This frozen delight is a great palate cleanser or can be transformed into a frozen shot by adding a jigger of rum or tequila to the prepared granita. A fun summer party offering.

3 cups watermelon pieces (master recipe, see p. 143), puréed

½ cup mint simple syrup (see p. 69)

▸ Mix the puréed watermelon into the sugar syrup until well blended.

▸ Pour into an 20 cm (8 in) square metal baking pan. Place in the freezer until ice begins to form at the edges of the pan, about 45 minutes.

▸ Using a fork, scratch up the mixture and freeze for another 45 minutes until icy at the edges of the pan and the overall texture is slushy.

▸ Stir to distribute the frozen portions evenly, and then freeze until solid, about 3 hours.

▸ Using a fork, scrape the granita down the length of the pan to form icy flakes. Working quickly, scoop the icy flakes into frozen shot glasses and serve.

Avocado and watermelon gazpacho

SERVES 4

I really enjoy cold soups in the summer so I love to experiment with what I find at the market. This Spanish delicacy takes on a lighter hue when using watermelon as the base to the soup. The avocado adds another level of texture and taste.

2 cups chopped seedless watermelon (master recipe, see p. 143)

1 clove garlic, minced

½ small onion

2 cups chopped tomatoes

1 cup chopped English cucumbers

1 jalapeño chilli pepper, minced

¼ cup lemon juice

2 tablespoons chopped fresh coriander

¾ teaspoon salt (or to taste)

Cracked black pepper to taste

1 avocado

⅛ teaspoon ground cumin

▸ Place the watermelon pieces in a blender and process until slightly chunky. Pour the processed watermelon into a large bowl and set aside.

▸ Using the same blender jug, add the garlic, onion, tomatoes, cucumber, jalapeño and 3 tablespoons of lemon juice and process until slightly chunky.

▸ Pour the tomato mixture into the watermelon mixture and mix well. Add coriander, salt and pepper.

▸ Refrigerate for 1–2 hours before serving to allow the flavours to blend.

▸ Just before serving, cut the avocado into small cubes and mix with the remaining lemon juice and the cumin.

▸ Serve the soup in bowls or shooter glasses topped with a spoonful of avocado.

To reduce the chance of eating a chunk of garlic, add a ¼ teaspoon of sea salt to the minced garlic. Using the back of a spoon, work the sea salt into the garlic to create a paste and then add to the mixture.

For the adventurous cook, grill the slices of watermelon before placing on bed of rocket.

Watermelon, feta and rocket salad with a balsamic glaze

SERVES 8

I love to surprise guests by turning plain watermelon slices into slightly spicy delicacies served over a bed of peppery rocket that has been tossed with a little lemon juice and olive oil.

1 tablespoon lemon juice

¼ cup olive oil

Salt and pepper

4 cups baby rocket

8 slices watermelon, cut into 3, rind removed (master recipe, see p. 143)

2 tablespoons chilli powder

1 cup crumbled feta cheese

¼ cup sunflower seeds, toasted

2 tablespoons balsamic glaze (see tip below)

▶ Whisk the lemon juice, olive oil, salt and pepper together in a medium bowl. Add the rocket and toss to coat with the mixture.

▶ Spread rocket over a medium-sized platter or fill a bowl.

▶ Sprinkle chilli powder over the watermelon pieces.

▶ Place the watermelon on top of the rocket and sprinkle with feta and sunflower seeds. Drizzle with balsamic glaze.

To make balsamic glaze: Boil balsamic vinegar until reduced by half.

Standing proudly in the Serengeti, Tanzania

THE YELLOWS

Butternut

Moving to South Africa was my butternut awakening as I was constantly being bombarded with the most original array of butternut recipes. So much so that it became a running joke in our family. The joke has led to some wonderful inventions.

Master recipe

Roasted butternut

MAKES 4 CUPS

4 cups, peeled and cubed butternut

1 teaspoon minced fresh ginger

½ tablespoon ground cinnamon

Sea salt and pepper to taste

3 tablespoons vegetable oil

▸ Preheat the oven to 350°F (180°C).

▸ Place the butternut cubes in a large mixing bowl.

▸ Add the ginger, cinnamon, seasoning and oil and mix well.

▸ Spread the butternut in a single layer in a flat-bottom baking dish and roast at for 30 minutes, or until soft and done.

HEALTH BENEFITS

Butternut is high in fibre, filling you up and helping to move fat through the digestive track.

Butternut is a complex carbohydrate, meaning it breaks down into glucose at a slow rate, giving the body a greater amount of energy throughout the day.

Butternut is loaded with beta-carotene and is a good source of vitamin A, vitamin C, manganese, magnesium and potassium.

BUYING AND STORING GUIDE

Look for a squash with a uniform, unblemished, dark beige skin. The skin should be hard and when the vegetable is picked up, it should feel dense.

Butternut stores well in a cool, dry place for a month or so. Keep out of plastic bags since the humidity makes them rot.

Butternut can be frozen either raw or cooked.

GREEN FINGERS

Butternuts are related to both cucumbers and melons.

Butternut seeds can be dried and planted directly in your garden.

The seeds can also be baked and used on salads, in toffee or eaten on their own as a snack.

Worms and pigs love the hard butternut skin.

Roasted butternut springrolls

MAKES 40

This was an experiment that I attempted when I had too much leftover butternut. It turned out to be a great recipe that can be kept on stand-by in the freezer for a quick and easy impressive treat.

1 teaspoon olive oil

2 tablespoons minced onion

1 teaspoon ground cumin

1 cup roasted butternut
(master recipe, see p. 153)

½ cup crumbled feta cheese

2 tablespoons chopped
fresh coriander

40 wonton wrappers

2 cups vegetable oil, for deep-frying

▸ Heat the olive oil in a pan and sauté the onion until translucent. Add the cumin and mix well. Remove from the heat.

▸ In a mixing bowl, combine the butternut, onion mixture, feta and coriander. Mash the mixture together with the back of a fork.

▸ Lay out individual wonton wrappers on a flat surface. Place 1 teaspoon of filling at the end of each wrapper and create a sausage shape with the filling.

▸ Roll the wrapper sides a quarter of the way up on each side then begin to roll the springroll. This will ensure that the stuffing does not escape. Seal the springroll with water. At this stage, the springrolls can be frozen.

▸ To serve, heat the oil in a wok. Deep-fry the springrolls in batches until golden brown. Make sure that the oil is not too hot or the rolls will open up. Drain on paper towel and serve hot with a sweet chilli sauce, a South African favourite.

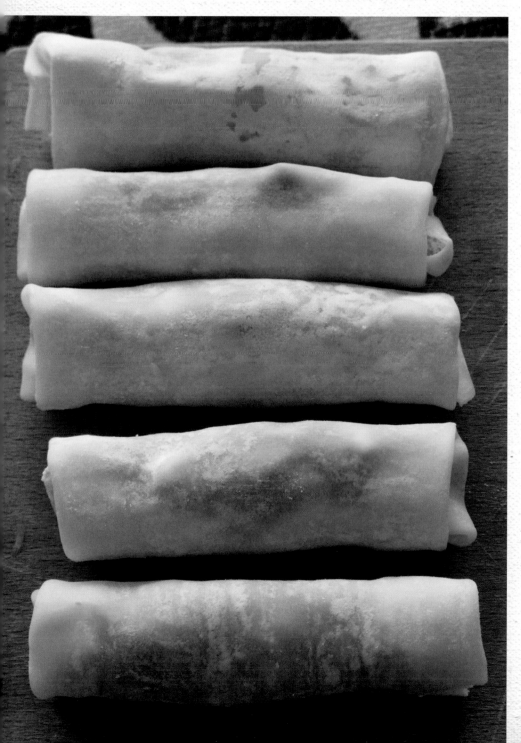

Butternut tarte tatin

SERVES 8

I used to avoid making tatins because I thought that they would be too difficult to control. I promise that I was very wrong. The sweet and salty combination of this recipe is a winner.

⅔ cup sugar

3 tablespoons water

⅓ cup butter

A dash of chilli flakes

2½ cups roasted butternut (master recipe, see p. 153)

1 sheet of frozen puff pastry, thawed

▶ Preheat the oven to 200°C (400°F). Set aside 8 ramekins.

▶ Dissolve the sugar in the water in a nonstick skillet over medium heat. Once a light caramel color is achieved, add the butter. Be careful when adding the butter as there will be a lot of bubbling and splattering.

▶ Divide the caramel between the 8 ramekins and sprinkle with some chilli flakes. Spoon the roasted squash over the caramel.

▶ Roll out the puff pastry to 1 mm thick and cut out rounds that are a little bigger than the opening of the ramekins.

▶ Place rounds of puff pastry over the squash and fold any extra pastry down the sides of the ramekin. Prick the pastry in many places with a skewer then place the ramekins on a baking sheet and bake for 30 minutes.

▶ Once cooked, allow to cool for 5 minutes, then invert onto a serving plate. Serve with a small rocket salad on top for an appetizer or cinnamon whipped cream (see p. 158) for a dessert.

Lentil and butternut bobotie

SERVES 4

My friend Bridget introduced me to this South African recipe as an alternate to the meat version. It reminds me of our shepherd's pie without the mashed potatoes. A true comfort food recipe!

2 cups brown lentils, cooked until just soft, no salt added.

1 tablespoon olive oil

1 medium onion, chopped

2 garlic cloves, minced

1 tablespoon minced ginger

2 tablespoons sweet chilli sauce

1 teaspoon cumin

½ teaspoon ground coriander

¼ teaspoon chilli powder

¼ teaspoon turmeric

2 cups roasted butternut (master recipe p153)

1 cup roasted tomatoes (master recipe p119)

2 tablespoons chopped flat leaf parsley

Custard

4 eggs

1 ½ cups milk

Salt and pepper to taste

4 bay leaves

▶ Pre-heat oven to 180C (350F)

▶ Soak lentils in a bowl of cold water. Before cooking, rinse until water runs clear.

▶ Cook lentils following the package instructions until just soft.

▶ Heat olive oil in a medium sized frying pan then sauté onion until soft. Stir in garlic, ginger, chilli paste, cumin, coriander, chilli powder and turmeric.

▶ Add roasted tomatoes and roasted butternut to mixture and cook for 4 minutes over medium heat until well combined.

▶ Spread a thin layer of lentils over the bottom of a 1 liter(1 quart) oven-proof dish.

▶ Cover with the tomato, butternut mixture then with a final layer of lentils.

▶ Mix together eggs, milk, salt and pepper.

▶ Pour custard mixture over lentils and spread bay leaves over the custard.

▶ Bake bobotie in the oven for 30 minutes or until custard is golden brown and set.

▶ Serve hot with a side of Mrs. Ball's chutney or Major Grey's chutney.

Butternut cake

SERVE 10–12

This is similar to a carrot cake, and is wonderfully moist. The glaze on top makes it a perfect afternoon treat with a freshly steeped cup of tea.

Roasted pumpkin or carrots may be substituted for the butternut.

⅓ cup vegetable oil

1 cup brown sugar

2 eggs

1½ cups roasted butternut (master recipe, see p. 153), mashed

1 cup flour

1 tsp baking powder

1 tsp bicarbonate of soda

¼ tsp salt

½ cup dried cranberries or raisins and chopped pecans

Lemon glaze

⅓ cup lemon juice

⅓ cup icing sugar

¼ cup honey

▶ Preheat the oven to 190°C (375°F). Grease a springform cake pan.

▶ Beat the oil, sugar and eggs together in a mixing bowl. Add the mashed butternut to the mixture.

▶ Sift the flour, baking powder, bicarbonate of soda and salt together. Add this to the squash mixture.

▶ Fold in the dried cranberries and chopped nuts, being careful not to overmix. Pour the mixture into the prepared cake pan and bake in the centre of the oven for 40–50 minutes.

Lemon glaze

▶ Place all the glaze ingredients in a small saucepan over low heat until the sugar has dissolved.

▶ When the cake is baked, remove it from the oven. Using a wooden skewer, poke holes all over the top of the cake and pour the hot glaze over the holes. Leave the cake in the pan for at least 30 minutes.

▶ Serve with some freshly whipped cinnamon cream.

To make cinnamon cream, add 1 teaspoon of sugar and ½ teaspoon ground cinnamon to every cup of whipping cream and whip into soft peaks.

Carrot

It was not until I began to grow my own carrots that I fully appreciated Bugs Bunny's favourite food. The sweetness of this root vegetable is a true delicacy when you wipe the soil from its skin and pop it in your mouth. There are truly so many ways to enjoy this kitchen staple.

Master recipe

Braised carrots

MAKES 2½ CUPS

500 g (1 lb) carrots

¾ cup water

1 tablespoon butter

½ tablespoon grated fresh ginger

½ tablespoon brown sugar (maple syrup can be substituted for the sugar)

Salt

▷ Cut the carrots into 5 cm (2 in) lengths.

▷ Place the carrots and water in a large saucepan and bring to a boil. Stir until all the water has evaporated.

▷ Add the butter and continue to stir the carrots until they are slightly softened, about 5 minutes.

▷ Add the ginger and sugar. Continue to stir until the carrots become well coated with the sweet ginger mixture. Cook until the carrots still have a little crunch, about 2–4 minutes.

▷ Finish off with some salt and serve.

BUYING AND STORING GUIDE

Look for firm, uniform coloured carrots with bright green tops.

Stay away from carrots that have yellow tips, shoots sprouting from the carrot and darkened stem ends. These are old and should be fed to your worms or your chickens, not your family!

Carrots are best stored without their tops. Rinse, place in a plastic bag and store in the coolest part of the fridge. Keep them moist so that they remain crisp.

Leave carrots in a bowl of cold water to revitalize them if they have become limp.

Carrots can be stored between layers of sand in a bin in a cellar, if you happen to have a cellar!

Carrots can also be stored in the freezer by scrubbing, cutting and blanching them in boiling water before freezing them.

HEALTH BENEFITS

Carrots are a hiker's first-aid kit! Use them mashed as a revitalizing face mask and as an antiseptic on cuts. Crunching on them also acts as a toothbrush and toothpaste in a pinch.

Carrots have high levels of beta-carotene, which converts into vitamin A to help with eyesight, anti-aging and the reduction of toxins in the body.

High in carotenoids, carrots are believed to help in the reduction of heart disease.

GREEN FINGERS

Short, stout carrots can be grown in containers while long, lean carrots need a veggie patch.

Carrots like to grow in full sun, but can adapt to partial shade.

The cooler the soil, the sweeter the carrot since starches convert to sugar as the temperature drops.

If making carrot juice, keep the carrot mash for making muffins rather than throwing it out.

Rather than throwing out carrot tops, use them to create a cold tea that can be stored in the fridge for up to 3 days. This is a great drink for detoxifying and helping with urinary problems.

Thai-flavoured spicy carrot soup

SERVES 6

I love Thai flavours, especially coconut and ginger, so this recipe is one of my favourites and is so easy to make. Other vegetables can also be used for this recipe, especially butternut.

1 tablespoon olive oil

1 onion, chopped

2.5 cm (1 in) piece of fresh ginger, sliced

1 tablespoons Thai red curry paste

2 cups braised carrots (master recipe, see p. 161)

4 cups chicken or vegetable stock

1 cup coconut milk

¼ cup chopped fresh coriander

▸ Heat the oil in a large saucepan and sauté the onion and ginger until the onion is translucent.

▸ Add the red curry paste and cook for 1 minute. Add the carrots and broth and cook for 10 minutes.

▸ Remove from the heat and put in a blender. Return the soup to the saucepan and stir in the coconut milk and coriander.

▸ Serve in bowls and garnish with coriander leaves.

Raw carrots also work in this recipe, but the cooking time will be longer. Butternut and other root vegetables can be substituted for the carrots.

Leftover coconut milk can be frozen and used later in another recipe.

This is a good recipe to use any water saved from cooking vegetables.

Carrot cake

SERVES 10–12

This carrot cake has the cream cheese frosting in the middle, making it easy to pack into a lunchbox. I love the idea that this is made from recycled carrots.

2 cups flour

1½ teaspoons bicarbonate of soda

1½ teaspoons ground cinnamon

½ teaspoon ground cloves

3 eggs

1 cup white sugar

½ cup brown sugar

⅔ cup oil

⅓ cup buttermilk

2 cups braised carrots (master recipe, see p. 161), finely chopped

¾ cup chopped walnuts

1 225g (8 oz) package of cream cheese

½ cup sugar

1 egg

1 tablespoon icing sugar, for dusting

▶ Preheat the oven to 180°C (350°F). Oil a springform pan.

▶ Sift the flour, bicarbonate of soda, cinnamon and cloves together in a medium bowl.

▶ In another bowl, beat the eggs, sugar and oil together. Once well blended, stir in the buttermilk and then stir in the carrots and the nuts.

▶ Using a rubber spatula, gently combine wet and dry ingredients.

▶ Pour half the batter into the prepared pan.

▶ In a separate bowl, mix together the cream cheese, sugar and egg. Pour the cream cheese mixture over the batter.

▶ Cover with the rest of the carrot batter. Using a spatula, make S motions though the batter to give a marbled effect to the cream cheese in the center of the carrot cake.

▶ Bake for 1 hour. Once done, remove from the pan and dust with icing sugar.

Raw grated carrots can be used in this recipe.

Carrot and cumin fritters

MAKES 6 MEDIUM FRITTERS

Fritters are so easy to make and are wonderful to have on their own or paired with grilled meat or a chopped salad.

1 cup braised carrots (master recipe, see p. 161), chopped

¼ cup onion, finely diced

1 clove garlic, minced

1 teaspoons ground cumin

½ teaspoon ground coriander

2 tablespoons chopped fresh coriander

Sea salt and white pepper

2 eggs, beaten

¼ cup buttermilk

½ cup flour

1 teaspoon baking powder

oil, for frying

▶ Combine the carrots, onion, garlic, ground cumin, ground coriander, fresh coriander and salt in a bowl and mix to combine.

▶ In a separate bowl, mix the eggs and buttermilk together. Stir into the carrot mixture.

▶ Gently mix in the flour and baking powder until just combined.

▶ Heat oil in a large frying pan over a medium to high heat and add spoonfuls of the mixture. Use a spatula to flatten the mixture into discs. Cook until golden on both sides.

▶ Drain on paper towels and keep warm in the oven while you fry the rest of the fritters.

▶ Serve with a cumin-scented Greek yoghurt.

Carrot hummus

MAKES ABOUT 1¾ CUPS

I love a good hummus with crudités or in a sandwich. Not only is it healthy but it also adds great flavour and added texture to a lunchbox sandwich.

Other vegetables, such as grilled red peppers (p. 113), also work well in this recipe.

1 cup braised carrots (master recipe, see p. 161)

400 g (14 oz) can chickpeas, rinsed and drained

2 tablespoons tahini

3 tablespoons olive oil

2 cloves garlic, minced

2 tablespoons lemon juice

1 teaspoon ground cumin

½ teaspoon chilli powder

¼ teaspoon sea salt, or more to taste

▸ Place all the ingredients in a food processor and whizz for several minutes until thick and smooth. You might have to stop once or twice to scrape down the sides of the bowl with a rubber spatula.

▸ Refrigerate in an airtight container for up to 3 days.

Corn

Corn on the cob has been a family favourite forever. Whether walking through the streets of Istanbul, having a lobster bake in Maine or a casual braai (barbecue) in Cape Town, corn has always been an important part of our menu.

Master recipe

Corn on and off the cob

SERVES 6

6 ears of corn, with husks but silk removed*

2 tablespoons salted butter

½ teaspoon chilli powder

1 teaspoon lime juice

Sea salt and pepper to taste

▸ Close up the husks and soak the corn in water for at least 30 minutes. Heat the grill.

▸ Mix the olive oil, chilli powder and lime juice together in a small bowl.

▸ Remove the corn from the water and place on the hot grill. Cook, turning the cobs constantly. The outer husks will get very crisp but the corn will cook and remain protected.

▸ Once the corn is cooked, 10–15 minutes, remove the husks and brush with the flavoured butter, olive oil and chili mixture. Serve immediately.

To remove the silk, carefully pull back the husks and pull out the silk.

HEALTH BENEFITS

Corn is high in fibre, which can be hard to digest but it is also effective in reducing constipation and hemorrhoids.

Folate (vitamin B9) found in corn is an important factor in the reduction of heart disease.

Since corn is full of vitamin B1, eating corn, in its natural form, helps to improve memory power and decreases the risk of Alzheimer's.

Cooking corn helps to release various anti-oxidants, which are beneficial in the prevention of eye disease as well as some types of cancer.

Corn helps to maintain blood sugar levels for Type 1 diabetics.

BUYING AND STORING GUIDE

Corn can be blanched and frozen on or off the cob.

Look for corn that has lots of golden silk sticking out the husk and a lovely green outer shell. A little secret to test the freshness is to burst a kernel with your finger to see how much milk comes out of it. The more milk, the tastier and fresher the corn.

The sugars convert to starch immediately after the corn is picked . The sooner you eat it the better. Within three days, sweet corn turns to mealy corn. If the bottom of the cob has turned brown, then the corn is more than 2 days old.

Keeping corn in the husk and in the fridge will help slow the starch conversion, but every day counts.

Parboiling corn for a minute then refrigerating the cobs for a day or so is effective in keeping it fresher for longer.

GREEN FINGERS

Corn needs lots of water, space and nutrients to be prolific.

Corn is a fantastic edible plant that can be planted in containers or in the garden.

Pigs and chickens love to eat the leftover cobs.

Cover the cobs with peanut butter and seeds to create a snack for garden birds.

Soak the black beans overnight to soften them. This reduces cooking time. For a gluten-free recipe, replace the bulgur wheat with quinoa.

½ cup cooked bulgur wheat

1 ½ cups boiling water

1 cup black beans, cooked, rinsed and drained

2 cups grilled corn (master recipe, see p. 169), removed from cob

1 red bell pepper, seeded and chopped

½ red onion, chopped

1 jalapeño chilli pepper, seeded and chopped

¼ cup lime juice

1 tablespoon olive oil

1 teaspoon ground cumin

¼ teaspoon chilli powder

¼ teaspoon ground coriander

Salt and pepper to taste

3 tablespoons chopped fresh coriander or flat-leaf parsley

Corn, bean and bulgur wheat salad

SERVES 6

This is a great salad to bring to a braai (barbecue). The ingredients are all so fresh and flavourful that they pair beautifully with any grilled meat or fish.

▶ To cook bulgur wheat, pour boiling water over bulgur wheat and allow to stand for 30 minutes.

▶ Drain bulgur through a strainer then pour into a medium salad bowl and fluff with a fork

▶ Add all the remaining ingredients to the bowl.

▶ Set aside for at least 15 minutes to allow the flavours to combine, then serve.

Corn blinis with lemon crème fraîche, smoked salmon and rocket

MAKES 22–24 COCKTAIL-STYLE BLINIS OR 6 LARGE ONES

This is my go-to-recipe when I want a quick but flavourful appetizer. It works beautifully with a cold glass of bubbly. Depending on the size of the blini, you can make big ones for an appetizer and mini ones for hors d'oeuvres. They also freeze beautifully.

Corn blinis

2 cups cooked corn kernels (master recipe, see p. 169), removed from cob

1 egg, beaten

¾ cup flour

1 teaspoon baking powder

½ teaspoon salt

½ teaspoon paprika

¼ cup milk

2 tablespoons chopped fresh coriander

Topping

½ cup crème fraîche

1 teaspoon lemon juice

zest of ½ lemon

200 g (7 oz) smoked salmon or trout, sliced

rocket leaves

cracked pepper

Corn blinis

▸ Blend 1 cup of corn in a blender to make it creamy.

▸ In a large bowl, mix the blended and whole corn with the egg.

▸ Sift the flour, baking powder, salt and paprika into another small bowl.

▸ Gently mix the flour mixture into the corn mixture, being sure not to over mix.

▸ Add milk and continue stirring. Add coriander and check seasoning.

▸ Brush a light coating of vegetable oil in a hot frying pan to prevent sticking. Pour in less than 1 tablespoon batter to make cocktail blinis or ¼ cup for large blinis.

▸ Once bubbles begin to appear on the surface, flip the blinis and cook the other side until light brown.

Topping

▸ Mix the crème fraîche, lemon juice and zest together in a small bowl.

To serve

▸ To serve, top the blinis with lemon-flavoured crème fraîche, smoked trout or salmon and a little rocket. A squeeze of lemon and cracked pepper to finish it off.

To store corn after it has been cooked, cut off of cob and refrigerate. You are more likely to reuse it if it is off the cob.

Creamed corn pudding

SERVES 4

This versatile recipe is great for using up corn from the previous night. The smoky flavour of the roasted corn gives an added dimension to the pudding.

1 tablespoon butter

2 tablespoons flour

¾ cup milk

1½ cups grilled corn (master recipe, see p. 169), removed from cob

¼ teaspoon mustard powder

2 pinches of cayenne pepper

2 eggs

1 tablespoon chopped fresh parsley

Sea salt and pepper to taste

▶ Preheat the oven to 180°C (350°F). Butter a 1-litre (1-quart) ovenproof dish.

▶ Create a béchamel sauce by melting the butter in a saucepan and then stirring in the flour. Cook over medium heat until it begins to whiten. Add the milk and whisk well so that it is free of lumps.

▶ Add the corn, mustard and cayenne pepper to the béchamel sauce and stir with a wooden spoon. Remove from heat and let cool slightly.

▶ Whisk the eggs in a separate small bowl and pour into the corn mixture.

▶ Finish off by adding parsley, salt and pepper to the mixture.

▶ Pour the batter into the buttered dish and bake for 25–30 minutes until puffed and slightly golden around the edges.

▶ Serve warm or at room temperature at a casual braai (barbecue) with a selection of grilled meats and a salad.

To turn this into a soufflé, separate 4 eggs and beat the yolks into the béchamel after you've added the corn. Whisk the egg whites to form peaks, and then fold them in. Sprinkle grated Parmesan cheese on top and bake.

Mealie bread

MAKES 1 LOAF

This is a recipe that I learned to make in South Africa. This is a typical bread that is made in the townships and in the countryside. Serve a warm slice with a slab of melting salted butter and you will feel as if you were in Africa.

1 cup grilled corn (master recipe, see p. 169) removed from cob

½ cup flour

½ cup mealie meal (fine polenta)

½ teaspoon salt

½ chilli pepper, seeded and chopped

1½ tablespoons oil

1 teaspoon instant yeast

½ cup warm water

▸ Mince the mealie (corn) kernels in a food processor.

▸ Stir the flour, mealie (corn) meal and salt together in a large bowl. Add the processed mealies to the flour mixture, then add the chili and 1 tablespoon of oil.

▸ Dissolve the yeast in the warm water in a small container.

▸ Make a well in the middle of the flour mixture and pour in the dissolved yeast and water. Using one hand, mix the ingredients together to create a sticky dough. Knead on a lightly floured surface for 3–5 minutes.

▸ Use the remaining ½ tablespoon of oil to grease a metal bowl. Place the dough into the prepared bowl, cover with a tea towel and set aside to rise for 30 minutes in a warm spot in the kitchen.

▸ Bring a large saucepan filled halfway with water to a boil, making sure that the metal bowl fits into the saucepan.

▸ Cover the bowl with foil and make a few small holes in the foil.

▸ Place the bowl into the boiling water, cover the saucepan with a lid and allow to steam for 1 hour. Make sure that the water does not touch the bread.

▸ Remove from pan and serve steaming hot with lots of butter!

Sweet potato

Sweet potato was once relegated to the Thanksgiving buffet table with a topping of marshmallows. Today, this humble root vegetable seems to be showing up in a vast array of recipes due to its health rating. My family and I have embraced its many redeeming qualities.

Master recipe

Baked sweet potatoes

SERVES 4

½ cup butter, softened

ground cinnamon

grated nutmeg

brown sugar

4 sweet potatoes, scrubbed and
pricked all over with a fork

▸ Preheat the oven to 200°C (400°F). Line a baking sheet with parchment paper or a silicone mat.

▸ Mix the butter with the cinnamon, nutmeg and brown sugar. Place the seasoned butter on a sheet of plastic wrap and roll into a log shape. Freeze.

▸ Place the sweet potatoes on the prepared baking sheet and bake for 40 minutes, or until fork tender and the skin is crisp.

▸ Cut open the cooked sweet potatoes and place a slice of seasoned butter in each one.

HEALTH BENEFITS

Sweet potatoes are high in potassium, which helps in the reduction of heart disease and muscle cramps.

Being low on the Glucose Index (GI) list, sweet potatoes are great for a diabetic diet.

To increase the benefits of beta-carotene (vitamin A) in sweet potatoes, some fat must be included in the recipe. That does not mean to go overboard!

Boiling or baking is better than steaming to achieve greater effects of the anti-oxidants and anti-inflammatory nutrients in sweet potatoes. These properties help in the prevention of heart disease, stroke, cancer, and delaying the progression of Alzheimer's disease.

Sweet potatoes are fat and cholesterol free.

BUYING AND STORING GUIDE

Choose firm sweet potatoes that have no cracks or soft spots and an even skin coloration.

Sweet potatoes should not be stored in the fridge since cold temperatures affect their taste.

A perforated brown paper bag in a cool, dark spot is the ideal storage location for sweet potatoes.

Cooked sweet potatoes in their jackets can be wrapped in plastic wrap and then placed in a freezer bag before freezing.

GREEN FINGERS

Sweet potatoes cannot be grown in regular containers but they can be grown in a stack of used tires, if you are feeling inspired. Be prepared for the sprawling plant.

Sweet potatoes like heat and well fertilized soil.

If you do not eat the skins, please be sure to feed them to the worms or the compost heap.

Sweet potato biscuits

MAKES 12 BISCUITS

These sweet potato biscuits cannot be resisted when they are hot out of the oven. I have taken on the South African tradition of lathering them with fresh butter, grated cheddar cheese and a topping of jam. A true delight.

2 cups cooked and mashed sweet potatoes (master recipe, see p. 177)

1½ cups milk

4 cups flour

1 tablespoon baking powder

1 teaspoon bicarbonate of soda

½ teaspoon salt

3 tablespoons sugar

1 cup cold butter, cubed

▶ Preheat the oven to 200°C (400°F). Line a baking sheet with parchment paper or a silicone mat.

▶ Mix the sweet potatoes and milk together in a mixing bowl until well blended.

▶ Sift the flour, baking powder and bicarbonate of soda together. Add the sugar.

▶ Using a fork, mix in the butter to create a mixture resembling coarse meal.

▶ Combine the sweet potato mixture with the dry ingredients to create a dough. Knead the dough gently 6 times on a well floured surface.

▶ Roll out the dough to 2.5 cm (1 in) thick and cut out rounds using a 5 cm (2 in) cookie cutter.

▶ Place the biscuits on the prepared baking sheet and bake for 15–20 minutes, or until golden brown.

▶ Serve with cinnamon whipped cream (see p. 158).

Roasted sweet potato, orange and ginger soup

SERVES 6–8

I am a soup lover so any leftover sweet potatoes are often translated into a soup for another meal. This is a refreshing recipe that is easy and quick to make.

1 tablespoon olive oil

½ cup minced onion

2 tablespoons minced fresh ginger

2 cloves garlic, minced

3½ cups baked sweet potatoes
(3 medium sweet potatoes,
master recipe, see p. 177)

4 cups chicken or vegetable stock

½ cup orange juice

¼ cup fresh cream

Sea salt and pepper to taste

▶ Heat the olive oil in a medium saucepan and fry the minced onions until translucent. Add the ginger and garlic and fry for a few more minutes.

▶ Add the sweet potatoes, stir and pour in the chicken or vegetable stock and orange juice. Cook for 20 minutes or until the sweet potato is falling apart.

▶ Allow the sweet potato mixture to cool before blending to a smooth mixture.

▶ Reheat the soup and serve in bowls with your choice of a drizzle of cream or sweet potato chips.

▶ This soup can also be made with uncooked sweet potato but the cooking time will be longer.

> *There are many varieties of sweet potatoes. I have noticed that the orange flesh ones are typically found in North America while the white flesh ones are often found in South Africa.*

Curry powder

1 tablespoon ground cumin

1 tablespoon ground coriander

1 teaspoon chilli powder

¼ tablespoon turmeric

Lamb curry

1 tablespoon turmeric

1 tablespoon grated fresh ginger

¼ cup white vinegar

1 kg (2 lb) lamb, cut into medium-sized cubes

3 tablespoons vegetable oil

½ cup minced onion

2 tablespoons thinly sliced fresh ginger

1 tablespoon minced garlic

½ yellow bell pepper, thinly sliced

½ red bell pepper, seeded and thinly sliced

½ cup cubed baked sweet potato (master recipe, see p. 177)

1 cup water

1 cup coconut milk

3 dried curry leaves

1 tablespoon chopped fresh coriander

Lamb and sweet potato curry

SERVES 6

Marinated lamb pieces are softened by the vinegar and ginger before they become part of a flavourful curry dish. I was first introduced to this dish in Kerala, the land of coconuts, in southern India.

▶ Mix all the curry powder ingredients together and set aside.

▶ Mix the turmeric, grated ginger and the vinegar together and marinate the lamb in the mixture for 1 hour.

▶ Heat 1 tablespoon of oil in medium skillet and sauté the lamb until browned. Remove to a bowl.

▶ In the same skillet, heat the remaining 2 tablespoons of oil and sauté the onion, sliced ginger and garlic together. Once softened, add the yellow and red bell peppers and cubed sweet potato. Sauté until the bell peppers begin to soften.

▶ Add 1 tablespoon of the homemade curry powder and ½ cup of the water. When the water has evaporated, add the lamb cubes and stir well.

▶ Add the rest of the water, cover, and continue to cook for 10 minutes.

▶ Add the coconut milk and dried curry leaves, cover and continue simmering for 10 minutes on medium heat until all the flavours have blended and the curry is cooked.

▶ Top the curry with fresh coriander and serve on a bed of couscous or basmati rice. Also good with kiwi chutney (p. 66) or plain yoghurt.

Buttermilk sweet potato waffles

MAKES 8 LARGE WAFFLES

I had some extra sweet potatoes in the fridge one morning so I decided to feed my children these waffles with the hidden ingredient. To my amazement, they all said that they were the best ever. They are now a family staple.

2 cups flour

2 teaspoons baking powder

1 teaspoon bicarbonate of soda

½ teaspoon ground ginger

¼ teaspoon grated nutmeg

1 teaspoon ground cinnamon

½ teaspoon salt

1 cup cooked and mashed baked sweet potato (master recipe, see p. 177)

2 cups buttermilk

2 eggs

1 tablespoon brown sugar

maple syrup, for serving

▶ Sift the flour, baking powder, bicarbonate of soda, ginger, nutmeg, cinnamon and salt together in a large bowl.

▶ In another bowl, mix together the mashed sweet potato, buttermilk, eggs and sugar.

▶ Pour the wet ingredients into the dry ingredients and carefully combine. Do not over mix. Set aside for 15 minutes.

▶ When bubbles begin to appear on the surface, it means the batter is ready for the waffle iron.

▶ Prepare waffles depending on your waffle maker.

▶ Serve piping hot with maple syrup.

If you happen to have leftover waffles, freeze them for future enjoyment.

Remember: Buttermilk can be made by adding 1 tablespoon of white vinegar to 1 cup of milk. Stir and set aside for a few minutes. The milk will begin to curdle.

Orange

The sweet tasting nectar of the orange has always been celebrated all over the world. I remember being surprised by the number of recipes calling for the use of oranges as a student at the Ritz Escoffier Culinary School.

Orange salad

SERVES 4

5 cardamom pods

2 cups water

1 cup sugar

1 cinnamon stick

4 long strips of lemon peel

5 oranges

▸ Remove the cardamom husks and crush the seeds.

▸ Place the water, sugar, ground cardamom, cinnamon and lemon peel strips into a pan. Bring to the boil and then simmer until the liquid is reduced to 1 cup (about 30 minutes).

▸ While the syrup is reducing, remove the peel from the oranges by cutting long segments of peel from the top to the bottom of the orange, opening up the orange like a flower. Save the peel segments to be candied (see p. 187).

▸ Cut the orange segments between the membranes to create half-moon pieces. Squeeze the juice out of the leftover membranes and either drink it or save for another recipe.

▸ Cool the syrup then strain and pour over the orange segments. Chill for at least 6 hours or overnight.

▸ Serve for breakfast or a refreshing luncheon dessert.

HEALTH BENEFITS

Oranges are full of vitamin C and flavonoids, which create strong immune systems and are important factors in fighting cancer.

It is best to squeeze your own orange juice since the pasteurizing process kills much of the phytonutrients.

Oranges are also good sources of vitamin A, vitamin B and folate, which aid in reducing wrinkles and enhancing eyesight.

Oranges are full of minerals, such as calcium and potassium, which help control heart rate and blood pressure.

The fibre in oranges helps keep the digestive tract healthy while also assisting in reducing cholesterol.

BUYING AND STORING GUIDE

Look for brightly coloured, heavy, firm oranges that have few wrinkles. The lighter the fruit, the less the juice and the drier the pulp.

Oranges are fine for a week or so at room temperature, but the ideal environment is loose in the fridge, with little moisture.

Orange zest is best stored in a sealed container in a cool, dry setting.

GREEN FINGERS

Orange peels in the garden act as a natural repellent to keep ants, flies, slugs, mosquitos and cats away.

If you need some kindling, use dried orange peels to get the fire started. The peels' natural oils are flammable.

Dried orange peels are ideal for a facial scrub or as an aromatic bath buddy.

Add orange or any citrus peel to sugar to give it a lovely flavour.

Candied orange peels dipped in dark chocolate

SERVES 6–8

I learned how to make these candied orange peels while at chef school in Paris. They are wonderful treats to have at the end of a meal with a steaming hot espresso.

peels from 3 oranges, pith removed

¼ cup grenadine

½ cup dark chocolate pieces

▸ Remove any additional pith from the peels and cut the peel segments into thin julienne strips.

▸ Blanch the peels in a small saucepan of boiling water for 2 minutes, then drain and place back into the saucepan with the grenadine. Bring the peels to a simmer and cook gently in the grenadine for a few minutes. Switch off the heat and allow to cool in the liquid.

▸ Warm the chocolate in a *bain-marie*. Once liquid, dip half of the peels into the chocolate and place on a baking sheet lined with parchment paper or a silicone mat. Allow to cool.

▸ Serve with coffee after dinner.

This recipe can also be made using other citrus peels.

Save squeezed out orange halves (from making orange juice), remove the insides and freeze to use as ramekins for this mousse recipe

Orange chocolate mousse

SERVES 4

This is not everyone's favourite but I cannot resist the mix of orange and chocolate. If you prefer a plain mousse, replace the orange juice with strong coffee and leave out the zest.

140g (5oz) bittersweet chocolate chunks

¾ cup sugar

zest of 1 orange

¾ cup + 1½ tablespoons orange juice

½ cup unsweetened cocoa powder

2 cups whipping cream, very cold

▶ In a medium size saucepan, melt the chocolate, sugar, orange zest, orange juice and cocoa powder together.

▶ Add extra juice, a teaspoon at a time, to the chocolate mixture, if it is too thick to mix into the whipping cream. Set aside to cool and refrigerate.

▶ While the chocolate mixture is cooling, whip the cream in a mixing bowl until stiff peaks form.

▶ Carefully fold the whipped cream into the chilled chocolate and orange mixture. Be sure that the chocolate is fully chilled and that the process is done in two steps. Mix a little whipped cream into the chocolate to start and delicately fold in the rest. Be sure not to over mix.

▶ Spoon the mousse into individual ramekins and refrigerate until ready to serve.

Baked orange, fennel and thyme chicken

SERVES 4

I love the flavours of citrus and fennel together. This dish is light and refreshing and can be made ahead for a weekday dinner or even for a casual dinner with friends.

For a stonger fennel flavour, add half Pernod and half vermouth.

4 chicken breast fillets, flattened

3 tablespoons flour

2 tablespoons olive oil

1 cup thinly sliced fennel bulb, plus fronds for garnishing

¼ cup vermouth

½ cup orange juice

¼ cup apple cider vinegar

1 teaspoon dried thyme

12–16 orange segments (master recipe, see p. 185)

4 sprigs of fresh thyme

▸ Preheat the oven to 180°C (350°F).

▸ Place the flour in a bowl and dredge the chicken in the flour.

▸ Heat the oil in a medium skillet and sauté the chicken pieces, making sure that they are browned on both sides.

▸ Transfer the chicken to an ovenproof dish.

▸ Add the fennel pieces to the skillet and sauté until softened, 4–5 minutes. Pour vermouth over the fennel and stir to pick up all the cooked pieces on the bottom of the pan. Once the vermouth has evaporated by half, pour in the orange juice, vinegar and thyme. Bring to a boil for 1 minute, then add the orange segments. Bring back to a boil and pour over the chicken.

▸ Finish cooking in the oven for 10 minutes. Garnish with fennel fronds and serve with rice or couscous.

Orange, beetroot, asparagus and watercress salad

SERVES 6-8

The key to this dish is not to mix the beetroot with the rest of the salad ingredients until just before serving, otherwise you will have a mass of pink salad, which is really only acceptable for a girl baby shower.

4 oranges, cut into segments (master recipe, see p. 185)

2 cups watercress

1 cup cooked asparagus (master recipe, see p. 19), cut into bite size pieces

2 tablespoons (½ log) goat's cheese, crumbled

4-6 medium roasted beetroot (master recipe, see p. 105), cut into pieces

Orange and mustard vinaigrette

¼ cup rice wine vinegar

¼ cup orange juice

2 tablespoons Dijon mustard

1 large clove garlic, minced

½ teaspoon honey

1 cup olive oil

Salt and freshly ground black pepper

Candied walnuts

¼ cup water

½ cup white sugar

1 teaspoon chilli powder

1 cup walnuts

Vinaigrette

▶ In a blender, combine the vinegar, orange juice, mustard, garlic and honey. With the motor running, add the oil in a continuous stream to create an emulsified dressing.

▶ Adjust salt and pepper to taste.

Candied walnuts

▶ Bring water and sugar to a boil in a small saucepan.

▶ Once the mixture begins to colour, remove from the heat and stir in the chilli powder and walnuts.

▶ Pour onto a baking sheet lined with parchment paper or a silicone mat. Once cooled, break into pieces and store in an airtight container.

To serve

▶ Place the orange segments, asparagus and watercress in a salad bowl. Pour over a little vinaigrette and toss until well combined.

▶ Add the beetroot and toss gently, being careful not to turn the salad pink.

▶ Sprinkle with crumbled cheese and candied walnuts.

Candied walnuts are wonderful snacks on their own, though addictive and a little decadent.

Orange and ricotta pancakes

SERVES 4

The ricotta adds a richer texture to these pancakes. I also prefer the coconut oil to regular oil since it adds sweetness. If you do not have coconut oil, vegetable oil works just as well.

1½ cups ricotta cheese

⅓ cup sugar

3 eggs

1 tablespoon orange zest

½ cup low-fat milk

1 cup flour

½ teaspoon baking powder

3 tablespoons coconut oil

▶ Whisk the ricotta, sugar, eggs, orange zest and milk together in a medium bowl.

▶ Mix in the flour and baking powder until just combined. If the batter is very thick, add a little extra milk.

▶ Heat 1 tablespoon of coconut oil in a large skillet over medium-low heat.

▶ Working in batches (and adding more oil to the skilled if necessary), pour a heaped tablespoon of batter into a hot pan. Cook until browned, about 3–4 minutes per side.

▶ Serve hot with orange slices and rooibos-infused orange syrup

Place the coconut oil jar in hot water to melt. Coconut oil is becoming a staple in many homes due to its health benefits, which outweigh all other oils.

Pancakes are ready to be flipped when their surface is covered in bubbles.

Rooibos-infused orange syrup

MAKES ¾ CUP

½ cup sugar

½ cup orange juice

½ cup water

2 rooibos tea bags

▶ Place all the ingredients in a saucepan and bring to a boil. Allow to boil for 10 minutes to create a syrup.

▶ Pour into a jug and serve warm alongside the pancakes.

Maple syrup is a good replacement if you do not have rooibos-infused orange syrup.

Peach

Peach season is a sign that summer has finally arrived. When I was growing up, baskets filled with these aromatic delicacies would flood into our kitchen, only to be transformed into the most scrumptious pies, crumbles and even breads.

Master recipe

Peeled peaches

SERVES 6

6 peaches	▶ Place the peaches in a large bowl.
boiling water	▶ Pour over enough boiling water to cover peaches fully.
¼ cup orange juice	▶ Leave in the water for a few minutes. Don't leave them too long as they will become mushy.
	▶ Using a knife, carefully peel off the skin. The boiling water will have helped to loosen the skin from the peach.
	▶ Slice the peaches and place in a serving bowl. Cover with orange juice to prevent discoloration.

BUYING AND STORING GUIDE

When checking for firmness, use your entire hand rather than just your fingers as peaches bruise easily.

Look for an even golden-yellow background with no green around the stem.

Peaches continue to ripen after being picked but cease to produce sugar once on your counter. To speed up the ripening process, place the fruit in a paper bag.

Smell the fruit to be sure that it has the aroma you want to taste in your mouth.

Look for the distinct crease to ensure full maturity.

Peaches can ripen on the counter or can be kept in a plastic bag in the refrigerator for up to 2 days.

Peaches can be peeled, sliced, placed on a baking tray, frozen and then stored in a sealable freezer bag for use up to 6 months. Overly ripe peaches can be chopped or puréed with a bit of acidity then frozen in an airtight container.

HEALTH BENEFITS

Peaches are high in fibre. They help keep intestines clean and reduce the risk of colon cancer.

Peaches are high in vitamin C, an antioxidant that helps keep skin looking young and the immune system primed.

Peaches contain beta-carotene, which is beneficial in creating vitamin A in our body, reducing the risk of cataracts.

The Chinese proverb 'may peaches prolong your life …' is based on the fact that peaches have a high level of potassium, which is important for a strong mind and body.

GREEN FINGERS

Save the peach pips, dry them out in a warm oven and use as decorative soil cover for potted plants.

Feed peach skins to worms or pigs.

Peach pips contain about 88 milligrams of cyanide. If you did happen to swallow one the hard outer shell would prevent you from ingesting the poison. At worst it would only give you a stomach ache.

Nectarines, apples, as well as mixed berries are a good substitute for peaches.

Peach and blueberry crumble

SERVES 6

I love crumbles and this crumble topping works for any fruit combo. Whenever I serve this dish for dessert, it is received with rave reviews.

3 cups peeled and sliced peaches (master recipe, see p. 195)

2 cups blueberries

1 tablespoon white sugar

2 tablespoons orange juice (can be used from the soaking peaches)

1 tablespoon Grand Marnier liqueur

2 teaspoons orange zest

1 cup sifted flour

2 cups rolled oats

1 cup brown sugar

1 teaspoon ground cinnamon

1 cup butter, cut into pieces

▶ Preheat the oven to 160°C (325°F).

▶ Put the peaches and blueberries in a shallow 2-litre (2-quart) baking dish.

▶ Combine the sugar, orange juice, Grand Marnier and orange zest and pour over the peaches and blueberries.

▶ Mix the flour, oats, brown sugar and cinnamon in a bowl. With one hand holding the bowl, rub in the butter until the mixture resembles coarse breadcrumbs.

▶ Spread the crumble mixture over the peaches and bake for 30 minutes, or until bubbling and golden.

▶ Serve warm with ice cream or whipped cream.

Ginger, peach and citrus popsicles

MAKES 6–8

Ice pops are the best way to use up fruit in the fridge. Whizz up fruit and juice in the blender, freeze it in individual cups or use the latest popsicle maker to have a healthy treat within minutes.

1 cup peeled and sliced peaches (master recipe, see p. 195)

2 teaspoons finely grated ginger

1 tablespoon lime juice

¼ cup orange juice

½ teaspoon honey

▸ Process all the ingredients until smooth.

▸ Pour into moulds and freeze.

▸ Serve to children and adults alike.

To turn these into adults-only treats, add a couple of jiggers of rum.

Remember that ginger can be stored in the freezer and removed just before it is needed.

Grilled mahi-mahi with a peach salsa

SERVES 4

When I was first introduced to mahi-mahi, I was told it was dolphin. I remember being horrified that my family would ever consider eating dolphin until I discovered that mahi-mahi has nothing to do with the cute dolphins we see swimming in the ocean. Any white flesh fish such as grouper or snapper can be substituted.

6 tablespoons soy sauce

3 tablespoons sesame oil

1 tablespoon grated fresh ginger

3 tablespoons lime juice

3 tablespoons honey

800gm (1.7 lbs) mahi-mahi

Be sure to ask the fishmonger if the fish you are choosing is endangered or over fished. I was sold White stumpnose as an alternative, only to discover that it is on the endangered list. I was not happy.

Peach salsa

¼ cup chopped red onion

½ cup chopped peeled peaches (master recipe, see p. 195)

½ red bell pepper, seeded and chopped

2 tablespoons lime juice

1 tablespoon minced fresh coriander

Sea salt and pepper to taste

▸ Mix the soy sauce, sesame oil, ginger, lime juice and honey together. Pour over the fish in a shallow dish and allow to marinate for 30 minutes.

▸ In a separate bowl, make the salsa by mixing all the salsa ingredients together. Set aside for 30 minutes before serving.

▸ Heat a griddle pan over medium high heat. Remove the fish from the marinade (reserve the marinade) and grill in pan.

▸ Pour the marinade into a small saucepan. Bring to a boil, then reduce the heat to low to allow the sauce to simmer.

▸ Glaze the fish with the sauce then serve with the peach salsa.

Peach and almond muffins

MAKES 12

I was in the habit of only making banana muffins. One day, when I had a basketful of overripe peaches, I decided that almond and peach muffins would be the perfect solution to saving the fruit and changing things up.

3 cups flour

½ cup almond flour

1 tablespoon baking powder

½ teaspoon bicarbonate of soda

½ teaspoon salt

2 teaspoons ground cinnamon

2 eggs

1¼ cups milk

½ cup sugar

1 cup butter, melted

2 cups peeled and chopped peaches (master recipe, see p. 195)

2 teaspoons almond essence

½ cup almonds, sliced

▸ Preheat the oven to 190°C (375°F). Grease a muffin pan.

▸ Sift the flours, baking powder, bicarbonate of soda, salt and cinnamon together in a large bowl.

▸ In a separate bowl, combine the eggs, milk, sugar and melted butter.

▸ Stir the wet ingredients into the dry ingredients, but be sure not to over mix.

▸ Mix the peaches, almond essence and almonds slices in a small bowl. Fold the peach mixture into the muffin batter.

▸ Fill the muffin cups with batter and bake for 20–25 minutes, or until cooked.

Almond flour is easily made by grinding up sliced peeled almonds.

Pineapple

A dessert for some and a breakfast treat for others, this tropical fruit is often seen on menus in Italy because Italians believe that pineapple helps in achieving weight loss. After a recent family trip through Italy, I very much doubt that pineapple could have helped with the caloric intake but, boy, was the fruit good!

Master recipe

Grilled pineapple

SERVES 4-6

1 pineapple

1 teaspoon chilli powder

▶ Cut off the pineapple greens, then slice off the peel. Remove individual eyes. Remove the centre core and slice into quarters.

▶ Sprinkle with chilli powder and grill over a hot grill or in a griddle pan for a few minutes on each side. leaving lovely brown grill marks.

▶ Serve with whipped cream as a refreshing and easy dessert.

BUYING AND STORING GUIDE

HEALTH BENEFITS

Pineapple's high levels of anti-oxidants, including vitamin C, helps in protecting against age-related eye problems as well as boosting the immune system.

The fibre in pineapples helps in curing constipation.

Beautiful skin devoid of age spots can be achieved with the help of the enzymes found in pineapples.

The vitamin C in pineapples helps to strengthen gums and reduce plaque, but the high level of sugar/fructose can erode the enamel so be sure to brush your teeth after eating this tropical fruit.

High in magnesium, pineapples help in the growth of bones in the young and to strengthen bones in the elderly.

When picking pineapples, choose ones that are plump, heavy, yellow in colour and have bright, shiny eyes.

Pineapples stop ripening the minute they are picked so be sure that the stem end of the fruit has a sweet, fragrant aroma.

This tropical fruit is not hardy and bruises easily. It cannot be stored for long since it is sensitive to the cold and quickly rots at room temperature.

A pineapple will keep for 2–4 days in the fridge in a perforated plastic bag or 4–7 days cut and covered in juice in a container in the fridge.

Pineapple can be frozen. Cut the fruit into pieces, cover it in juice and freeze for up to 6 months. There is some loss of flavour so I would recommend eating it fresh rather than freezing it.

GREEN FINGERS

Pineapple plants take 18–22 months to bear one single fruit on a large stem. The fruit gets progressively smaller every year so a plant can only be harvested over a two to three year period.

When cooking with pineapples, be aware that it has an enzyme called bromelain, which acts as a tenderizer. When added to protein, it can over-tenderize a dish if you're not careful. Cooked pineapple and its juice does not have the same effect.

Rather than throwing out the skin, slice it into thin strips and use as cocktail stirrers for a tropical punch.

Use the outer skin as a bowl for a salad bowl.

Leave pieces of pineapple in the garden to attract chameleons.

Buttermilk French toast with grilled pineapple

MAKES 6–8 SLICES

Breakfast is the most important meal of the day so make it count with this French toast recipe which can be whipped up in the morning with very little mess.

2 cups buttermilk

4 eggs

1 teaspoon ground cinnamon

2 tablespoons coconut oil (or vegetable or sunflower oil)

6–8 slices day-old bread

grilled pineapple (master recipe, see p. 203) and maple syrup, for serving

▶ Whisk the buttermilk, eggs and cinnamon together in a flat, shallow bowl.

▶ Dredge bread slices in the buttermilk mixture allowing a few minutes so that the bread is impregnated with the mixture.

▶ Heat the oil in a nonstick skillet over medium-high heat.

▶ Transfer the bread to the skillet using a slotted spatula and fry until slightly puffed and golden brown. Turn over and fry the other side.

▶ Transfer to a baking sheet and keep warm in the oven until all the slices are cooked.

▶ Serve French toast with slices of grilled pineapple and maple syrup.

Grilled pork tenderloin with a pineapple salsa

SERVES 6

Pork tenderloin is not always easy to find in South Africa, but when I do find it, I often grill it with this salsa as an accompaniment. It is so simple yet so good.

Salsa

12 slices grilled pineapple
(master recipe, see p. 203)

1 red bell pepper, seeded
and chopped

1 jalapeño chilli pepper,
seeded and chopped

1 mango, peeled, seeded
and chopped

½ red onion, chopped

1 tablespoon lime juice

½ teaspoon lime zest

2 tablespoons chopped
fresh coriander

Sea salt and pepper to taste

Pork

2 pork loins

¼ cup olive oil

½ tablespoon chilli powder

1 tablespoon brown sugar

¼ cup soy sauce

1 tablespoon minced garlic

1 tablespoon minced ginger

Salsa

▸ Place all the salsa ingredients in a medium bowl. Mix and set aside for at least 30 minutes before serving with the grilled pork.

Pork

▸ Combine olive oil, chilli powder, brown sugar, soy sauce, garlic and ginger in a bowl. Marinate the pork in this mixture for at least 1 hour.

▸ Heat the grill and barbecue the pork over medium heat, being careful not to burn the loins.

▸ Once cooked, serve slices of pork topped with the salsa.

As with most meats, allow the pork to rest for 5–10 minutes before slicing to help retain the juices. This cut is best sliced on a diagonal.

Pineapple cooler

SERVES 6

Why let any extra grilled pineapple slices go to waste when this refreshing drink is so easy to make. It is a true mix of tropical beach meets urban bar, with or without the alcohol.

5 full pineapple slices
(master recipe p. 203)

1 cup mint simple syrup (see p. 69)

ice cubes

2 cups soda water

fresh mint leaves, for garnishing

▶ Pulse the pineapple and sugar syrup together in a blender to obtain a lumpy consistency.

▶ Strain the mixture into a pitcher and add ice and soda water. Garnish with mint leaves.

You can also serve this with a jigger of dark rum per glass.

Pineapple upside-down cake

SERVES 8

The sweet caramelized pineapple slices are the star attraction of this cake since they become the topping. I often serve this cake with a dollop of whipped cream.

¼ cup butter

⅔ cup brown sugar

3 tablespoons rum or vanilla essence

8 full slices of grilled pineapple, quartered (master recipe, see p. 203)

2 cups flour

2 teaspoons baking powder

¼ teaspoon salt

⅔ cup sugar

¾ cup coconut milk

1 egg

⅓ cup melted butter

▶ Preheat the oven to 180°C (350°F).

▶ Melt the butter, brown sugar and 2 tablespoons of rum or vanilla essence in a saucepan.

▶ Once melted, pour into the bottom of a round 23 cm (9 in) baking pan.

▶ Place the grilled pineapple slices in a concentric, slightly overlapping pattern in the base of the pan.

▶ Sift the flour, baking powder and salt together in a bowl. Add the white sugar.

▶ In the bowl of an electric mixer, mix the coconut milk, egg, white sugar, melted butter and 1 tablespoon of rum or vanilla together until well blended.

▶ Gently mix the dry ingredients into the wet ingredients, being careful not to over mix.

▶ Pour the batter evenly over the pineapple slices. Bake for about 40 minutes, or until a toothpick inserted in the centre comes out clean. Remove from the oven and allow to cool slightly.

▶ Run a knife around the edges of the cake pan, place a plate over the pan and gently flip it over so that the caramelized pineapple slices sit on top.

▶ If some slices stick, carefully scoop up the pieces and place them back on the cake.

▶ Serve with a dollop of whipped cream.

For a change, substitute other fruit, such as plums and blueberries, for the pineapple.

Lioness and her cubs out on an excursion near Zarafa Camp, Chobe Park, Botswana.

THE WHITES

Cauliflower

This vegetable always makes me smile since it is one that my husband refuses to eat even though, when we were dating, he pretended that he loved the family favourite of cauliflower with cheese sauce. The minute I said "yes", he put his foot down and has not eaten the dish since.

Master recipe

Roasted cumin-scented cauliflower

SERVES 3–4 AS A SIDE DISH

Ingredients	
2 tablespoons olive oil	▸ Preheat the oven to 200°C (400°F).
1 teaspoon cumin seeds	▸ In a medium mixing bowl, stir the olive oil, cumin seeds, ground coriander, lemon juice and salt together.
1 teaspoon ground coriander	
1 teaspoon lemon juice	▸ Add the cauliflower florets and coat with the oil mixture.
½ teaspoon sea salt	▸ Place on a baking sheet and roast for 20 minutes, or until the florets are soft and slightly brown. Stir the cauliflower after 10 minutes of cooking so that the pieces brown evenly.
1 medium head of cauliflower, cut into florets of similar size	

HEALTH BENEFITS

Full of anti-oxidants, cauliflower contains vitamin C, magnesium and beta-carotene to fight off the free radicals associated with cancer, cardiovascular disease and aging.

Cauliflower is also full of anti-inflammatory elements, including vitamin K which, if ingested on a regular basis, will help in decreasing the risk of arthritis, diabetes, obesity and other inflammation-related diseases.

The fibre in cauliflower is highly effective in assisting in the protection of stomach and intestines from ulcers and cancers.

To keep the body properly hydrated and the heart in sync, cauliflower offers an excellent source of potassium.

The folate in cauliflower is the anti-oxidant responsible for helping to ensure a reduced number of birth defects.

BUYING AND STORING GUIDE

Cauliflower heads should be cream-coloured with compact florets and no brown spots. The leaves that envelop the head should look fresh, green and crisp.

Cauliflower heads can last up to two weeks in the fridge if they come fresh from the market or one week if bought at a store.

Because of its size, cauliflower is often easier to use once cut into florets and stored in a plastic bag in the fridge. Slice up the stems as well as the florets – they're delicious roasted.

The best way to store cauliflower for an extended period is to blanch the florets and sliced stems in boiling water. Cool in ice water and then spread on a baking sheet to freeze. Once frozen, repack the florets in airtight freezer containers.

GREEN FINGERS

Cauliflower, a cruciferous vegetable, does not grow well in containers and can be difficult to grow in climates where summers are hot.

Sun and heat are responsible for making cauliflower florets bitter.

Though found year round, cauliflower is most often at its best in the fall and winter.

Cauliflower leaves and stem ends are perfect for worm bins, pigs, chickens and a compost heap.

Thai-flavoured cauliflower

SERVES 4

*I love the way that cauliflower is so versatile. Whatever spices are used, this
main ingredient is very accepting and seldom fails to impress.*

Uncooked florets can
be used, but the cooking
time will be longer.
Onion, garlic and ginger are the
base of Indian, Thai, Creole and
so many other global foods.
Ginger can be stored in the
freezer as is, no wrapping
necessary.

1 tablespoon coconut oil

½ cup thinly sliced onion

2 teaspoons minced garlic

1 tablespoon minced ginger

1 teaspoon red curry paste
(or more depending on
level of heat you want)

1 cup coconut milk

2 tablespoons tamari or soy sauce

1 tablespoon lime juice

1 teaspoon lime zest

1 stalk lemon grass, bruised

1½ cups roasted cauliflower
(master recipe, see p. 213)

½ cup fresh coriander
leaves, chopped

▸ Heat the oil in a large skillet and
fry the onion until softened.

▸ Add the garlic and ginger and
continue cooking for an additional
minute.

▸ Add the curry paste and cook for
a few more minutes.

▸ Add the coconut milk, tamari,
lime juice and zest, and the lemon
grass and bring to a boil.

▸ Reduce the heat to medium-low
and add the cauliflower. Simmer
all the ingredients until the
cauliflower is heated through.

▸ Top with coriander leaves and
serve.

Cauliflower pakora

SERVES 6–8

This recipe is inspired by my last trip to India. I spent an afternoon touring Old Delhi experiencing street food. This was one of my favorite recipes because almost any vegetable can be used.

There is no substitute for chickpea flour in this recipe if you want a truly authentic pakora. Raw cauliflower can be used for this recipe, but the cooking time will need to be extended.

1 cup chickpea flour

1 teaspoon baking powder

A pinch of chilli powder

1 tablespoon chopped fresh coriander

½ teaspoon ground cumin

½ teaspoon turmeric

½ cup water

2 cups roasted cauliflower florets (master recipe, see p. 213)

1 cup oil for frying

▶ Mix the flour, baking powder, chilli, coriander, cumin and turmeric together. Slowly add water to make a batter that is not too thick, but not too watery either.

▶ Heat the oil in a saucepan.

▶ Drop the florets into the batter and stir gently until all the pieces are well coated.

▶ You can also do one floret at a time, depending on your mood.

▶ Fry a few florets at a time in the hot oil until a golden brown colour is achieved. Do not allow the oil to get too hot, otherwise the outside will cook while the pastry inside remains raw.

▶ Remove with a slotted spoon and drain on paper towel.

▶ Serve as an appetizer with a glass of bubbly.

Roasted cauliflower purée

SERVES 4

Puréed vegetables can be so good when paired with a grilled piece of fish or meat. The leeks add another dimension to this not-quite-smooth purée.

1 garlic clove, minced

2 cups roasted cauliflower
(master recipe, see p. 213)

1 cup vegetable or chicken broth

1 tablespoon butter

1 tablespoon crème fraîche

Salt and pepper

2 leeks, white part only, thinly sliced

1 tablespoon flour

1 tablespoon butter

Crème fraiche can be replaced with thick Greek yoghurt.

Use stock alone to offer a vegan alternative.

Cauliflower purée

▸ Place garlic, cauliflower and stock in a medium saucepan.

▸ Bring to a simmer and cook until garlic and cauliflower are soft.

▸ Transfer the cauliflower mixture to a food processor, reserving the cooking liquid for later.

▸ Add the butter and crème fraîche to the cauliflower mixture and blend until nearly smooth. Add small amounts of stock until the desired consistency is achieved. Remember you can add but cannot take out any ingredients!

▸ Season with salt and pepper to taste.

Leeks

▸ Before serving, toss the sliced leeks in the flour.

▸ Heat a little oil to medium-high in a wok and drop in floured leeks. Fry until they turn brown. Remove to a paper towel and drain. Add some salt.

To serve

▸ Place the cauliflower purée in a saucepan and heat slowly. Add 1 tablespoon of butter at the end to add richness. Re-heating can also be done in a microwave.

▸ Place a mound of cauliflower purée on the plate and garnish with crispy leeks.

Cauliflower mac and cheese

SERVES 6

Mac and cheese is a childhood favourite so why not give it some added nutrition by hiding a few cauliflower florets in the cheese to create a full meal. This is basically cauliflower and cheese sauce with some added carbs.

2 cups elbow macaroni or penne pasta

3½ cups milk

4 tablespoons butter

6 tablespoons flour

3¼ cups grated extra-sharp Cheddar cheese

1 cup Emmenthal cheese

1 tablespoon salt

¼ teaspoon black pepper

½ teaspoon ground nutmeg

½ teaspoon mustard powder

1 cup roasted cauliflower (master recipe, see p. 213)

¼ cup fresh white breadcrumbs

1 tablespoon grated Parmesan cheese

1 teaspoon olive oil

▶ Preheat the oven to 180°C (350°F).

▶ Bring a large saucepan of water to a rolling boil. Cook the pasta until al dente. Reserve 1 cup of pasta water before draining the noodles.

▶ Melt the butter in a medium-sized saucepan and add the flour. Cook, stirring constantly, over low heat for 2 minutes, or until mixture begins to look opaque.

▶ Whisk in the milk and continue to stir over medium heat until the sauce begins to thicken. You have now created a béchamel sauce!

▶ Reduce the heat and stir in 3 cups of the Cheddar, the Emmenthal, salt, pepper, mustard and nutmeg until melted and well blended.

▶ Add the cooked pasta and stir to coat. Carefully add the cauliflower.

▶ If the mixture is too thick, add a little of the reserved pasta water.

▶ Pour the mixture into a 3-litre (3-quart) ovenproof dish.

▶ Mix the breadcrumbs, remaining Cheddar, the Parmesan cheese and oil together. Sprinkle on top of the prepared pasta.

▶ Bake for 20 minutes in the oven, or until the sauce is bubbly and the breadcrumbs are brown and crispy.

Mushroom

For years, I was the only one in my family to like mushrooms. One day out of the blue, my son Patrick started to devour these little fungi. He is mad about my mushrooms, to the point that I have to have them marinated and ready for him when he comes home from university.

Master recipe

Roasted mushrooms

Remember: To make a garlic paste, use sea salt and the back of a spoon to mash the garlic and salt together. Then mix the garlic paste into the olive oil.

100 g (¼ lb) mushrooms (any mushrooms will do, but button, bella, portabello and brown mushrooms work best)

½ cup olive oil

2 tablespoons sea salt

3 cloves garlic, sliced

1 tablespoon Herbes de Provence

fresh thyme

▸ Preheat the oven to 180°C (350°F).

▸ Cut the mushrooms into bite-sized pieces.

▸ Add olive oil, salt, garlic and Herbes de Provence and toss together.

▸ Transfer to a baking sheet and sprinkle fresh thyme over the mushrooms. Bake for 30–40 minutes, or until the mushrooms are fully cooked.

Be sure not to crowd mushrooms when roasting otherwise they will boil in the water they release rather than roast.

HEALTH BENEFITS

Mushrooms are the only edible plants that produce vitamin D when exposed to sunlight or ultraviolet light.

Portabello and button mushrooms are believed to have extremely high anti-oxidant levels to combat disease.

Due to a high level of an essential trace mineral called selenium and vitamin E, mushrooms are effective in reducing the effects of free radicals on healthy cells.

Did you know that a strong mind and heart is the positive effect that mushrooms have on humans due to their high content of potassium?

Mushrooms are 90% water and do not contain any fat, sodium or cholesterol, making them an ideal healthy food choice.

BUYING AND STORING GUIDE

When buying mushrooms, look for firm, bruise-free heads with soft springy stems that have not dried out.

Mushrooms do not store well and should be eaten within days of being purchased.

If buying from a farmer's market, keep mushrooms in plastic bags in the fridge. If store bought, keep mushrooms in their original packaging until ready to use.

To clean mushrooms, wipe with a damp towel or pass under running water then pat them dry. Do not soak as they will absorb the water and become soggy.

Mushrooms can be sautéed in olive oil or butter, cooled and then placed in sealed containers in the freezer. Their colour and texture will change when frozen. They can also be canned, pickled or dried for storage purposes.

GREEN FINGERS

There are over 1.5 million species of mushrooms on this planet, but very few are edible. Remember to be responsible when foraging for mushrooms and be sure that you have a knowledgeable fungi leader.

Mushrooms are not fruits or vegetables but rather fungi.

Mushrooms can be grown at home in dark, damp, well-ventilated areas such as cupboards, basements or cellars. Once a growing medium is chosen and spawns (seedlings) are bought, the process is simple.

Oyster mushrooms can be grown on used diapers. This new discovery permits 90% of a disposable diaper to be decomposed within 2 months rather than over centuries in a crowded landfill.

Before any leftover white wine spoils in the fridge, pour it into ice trays and freeze to use in sauces and other recipes.

You can also use raw mushrooms, but they will need to be cooked for longer to evaporate the water.

Mushroom cups

MAKES 12 CUPS

This is a good recipe to use up both cooked mushrooms and old bread. It is also a fun recipe to do with kids or beginner cooks in the kitchen. They might even begin to like mushrooms!

¼ cup chopped onion

1 teaspoon minced garlic

1 cup chopped cooked mushrooms (master recipe, see p. 221)

¼ cup white wine (broth if you do not want to use alcohol)

½ cup whipping cream

2 eggs, beaten

1 teaspoon dried thyme

A pinch of cayenne pepper

1 teaspoon lemon juice

Salt and pepper

▸ Preheat the oven to 180°C (350°F). Grease and set aside a mini-muffin pan.

▸ Heat the oil in a medium skillet and sauté the onion until softened. Add the garlic and cook for 2–3 minutes over medium heat.

▸ Add the mushrooms and continue cooking until all the liquid has evaporated. Add the wine, bring to a boil and reduce until almost all the wine has evaporated.

▸ Stir in the cream and cook until thickened. Remove from the heat, allow to cool then add the egg, thyme, cayenne pepper and lemon juice. Season to taste with salt and pepper.

▸ Spoon the mixture into the greased mini muffin pan and bake for 10 minutes at 180°C (350°F).

▸ Serve garnished with a sprig of thyme.

Check out how to make breadcrumbs on p. 30.

Use reserved cooking water from other vegetables or chicken broth for these croquettes.

Leek and mushroom croquettes

MAKES ABOUT 16

This tapas-style hors d'oeuvre is most often prepared with meat, but I decided that a garlic, leek and mushroom combo would be just as good. The key is to make the filling firm enough to roll and fry.

4 tablespoons butter	Melt the butter in a medium skillet and then add the leeks and garlic. Cook until wilted.
½ cup chopped leeks, white part only	Stir in ½ cup of the flour and cook for a few minutes, but be careful not to let it brown.
1 teaspoon minced garlic	Whisk in the milk, followed by the broth. Simmer over low heat until thickened. Add the mushrooms, thyme and seasoning.
1 cup flour	
¾ cup milk	Spread the mixture in a shallow glass dish and refrigerate. Once cool and quite solid, form the mixture into 16 or so balls and place on a baking sheet lined with parchment paper or a silicone mat.
½ cup vegetable stock	
1 cup roasted mushrooms (master recipe, see p. 221), diced into minute pieces	Prepare three bowls with one of the following ingredients in each: 2 beaten eggs, the remaining flour and the breadcrumbs.
1 teaspoon dried thyme	Roll each ball into an oblong shape and dredge in flour, eggs and then breadcrumbs. Return to the baking sheet and repeat with the remaining balls.
Salt and pepper to taste	
2 eggs	Heat the oil to a maximum of 180°C (350°F) and fry the breaded oblong balls in batches. When the croquettes are browned on all sides, remove with a slotted spoon and drain on paper towels.
1-1 ½ cups breadcrumbs	
2 cups vegetable oil, for deep-frying	Serve immediately since these croquettes will not keep well in a warm oven.

Grilled ostrich steaks with a wholegrain mustard and mushroom sauce

SERVES 6

The creamy mustard and mushroom sauce complements the lean and healthy grilled ostrich. If ostrich is not readily available, it can be replaced with a beef fillet.

¼ cup olive oil

2 cloves garlic, minced

1 tablespoon steak spice

6 ostrich steaks

Mustard and mushroom sauce

1 tablespoon olive oil

⅓ cup finely chopped onion

2 shallots, minced

½ cup white wine

1 cup chicken or beef stock

2 tablespoon Maille wholegrain mustard

1 cup heavy cream

½ cup finely chopped cooked mushrooms (master recipe, see p. 221)

▸ Mix the ¼ cup olive oil, garlic and spices in a plastic bag, then add the steaks. Set aside for at least 30 minutes.

Mustard and mushroom sauce

▸ In a medium frying pan, heat 1 tablespoon olive oil and sauté the onion and shallots until translucent. Add the wine, bring to a boil and allow the mixture to reduce by half.

▸ Add the stock and mustard, allowing it to cook for 2–3 minutes, then add the cream and mushrooms. Bring the sauce to a boil and cook for another 2–3 minutes to thicken. Set aside until the steaks are cooked.

▸ To cook the steaks, heat a grill to medium-high. Grill the steaks until the proper stage of doneness is achieved. Remove from the heat and serve with a coating of the warm sauce.

Ostrich is not a meat that can be served well done. For medium-rare, grill maximum 4 minutes per side depending on thickness, and 6 minutes per side for medium.

Mushroom and chickpea fries with roasted tomatoes and basil

SERVES 6

A great change to regular fries. A sprinkle of truffle oil is also a delightful addition to this appetizer or side dish served with roasted tomatoes (see p. 119)

2 cups milk

1 teaspoon salt

2 cups chickpea flour

½ cup roasted mushrooms
(master recipe, see p. 221)

1 cup grated Parmesan cheese

¼ cup olive oil

▸ Bring the milk and salt to a boil in a saucepan over medium heat.

▸ Turn down the heat and whisk a constant stream of 1 cup of the chickpea flour into the milk. Whisk in the final cup of chickpea flour, without stopping.

▸ Change to a wooden spoon and continue mixing while adding the mushrooms, followed by the Parmesan cheese. Cook for a few minutes over low heat until the mixture begins to form a ball.

▸ Spread out the mixture in a medium-sized pan to the thickness of a fry. Allow to cool and then slice the mixture into rectangular batons resembling thick fries.

▸ Heat half of the olive oil and fry the individual batons until golden on all sides. Add additional oil as needed.

▸ Serve stacked with a small dipping dish of warm roasted tomatoes mixed with some chopped basil.

Keep parmesan cheese rinds in the freezer and add to soups or sauces when an added boost of flavour is needed.

Banana

A banana is one of the few fruits that never has time to spoil in my kitchen. I sometimes have to hide this fruit in a cupboard to be able to make my mother's much-loved banana bread.

Master recipe

Bananas in spiced syrup

SERVES 4

1 cup water	▷ Place the water and sugar in a small saucepan and bring to a boil. Reduce by half.
1 cup sugar	
1 cinnamon stick	▷ Add the cinnamon, cloves and lemon juice and continue boiling for 5 minutes. Remove from the heat and allow to cool.
4 whole cloves	
1 teaspoon lemon juice	▷ Cut up the bananas and add to the syrup. Set aside for 15 minutes before serving.
3 bananas	
	▷ Serve with ice cream and chopped peanuts.
	▷ Freeze leftover banana slices in containers without the poaching sauce.

HEALTH BENEFITS

Potassium-rich bananas are natural brain boosters as well as heart and blood pressure regulators.

Potassium also helps to neutralize our intake of sodium, thereby sustaining levels of calcium to support bone strength.

Bananas have enough dietary fibre to regulate digestion and maintain blood sugars.

High in magnesium, vitamins B6 and B12, this popular fruit helps to reduce levels of nicotine in your body, which is ideal if you or a friend are looking to quit smoking.

BUYING AND STORING GUIDE

This is one fruit that is best bought organic and fair trade certified to reduce the negative effects of regular banana cultivation, which includes leaching of high amounts of chemicals into the environment and exploitation of employees.

It is best to buy bananas when they are 75% yellow with green at both ends.

Keep bananas on their own to prevent the ethelyne gas they release from affecting the ripening of other fruits.

GREEN FINGERS

Before throwing out a banana peel, rub it on any mosquito bite or swelling to give relief.

Cut up peels and feed them to your worm farm. Less trash, more mash for the garden.

Rub peels on houseplant leaves to give them a brilliant shine.

Banana peels whizzed in a blender with water makes a great fertilizing potion for flowering plants including orchids and roses.

Peanut butter and banana smoothie

MAKES 2 LARGE OR 4 SMALL SMOOTHIES

This is a meal in a glass, serving up protein and lots of fibre and potassium to give you a natural boost for the day. Keep some bananas in the freezer for this quick pick me up.

2 ripe frozen bananas
or full bananas

2 cups low-fat milk

¼ cup honey

½ cup peanut butter

A handful of ice cubes

▶ Combine all the ingredients in a blender until the mixture is smooth and frothy. Serve immediately.

Bananas freeze well. Cut up ripe bananas and freeze flat in a container or freezer bag.

Banana bread

MAKES 1 LOAF

This is a family favourite that uses up ripe bananas. This recipe is as good in bread form as it is in muffin form. I do not like nuts in my muffins, but feel free to add them if you feel inspired.

½ cup butter, at room temperature

1¼ cups sugar

2 eggs

1 teaspoon vanilla essence

2 cups flour

1 teaspoon baking powder

1 teaspoon bicarbonate of soda

1 cup sour cream

1 cup bananas (master recipe p. 229), mashed (2–3 bananas)

▶ Preheat the oven to 180°C (350°F). Grease the bottom and sides of a loaf pan (or muffin pan) with butter.

▶ Beat the butter and then add the sugar. Once well creamed, add the eggs, one at a time, then add the vanilla.

▶ In a separate bowl, sift the flour, baking powder and bicarbonate of soda together. Add to the butter and egg mixture.

▶ Cream the mashed bananas and sour cream together in a separate bowl. Once mixed, add to the flour and butter mixture.

▶ Pour the mixture into the prepared pan and bake for about 50 minutes, or until a skewer inserted in the centre comes out clean.

My grandmother's trick was to keep empty butter wrappers in the fridge to use for greasing baking dishes.

Banana fritters with chocolate sauce

MAKES 12 FRITTERS

These are bite-sized bananas on a stick, which I love to dip in chocolate sauce. I first tried these in Asia as a snack and fell in love with them. My gourmand side decided that ice cream and chocolate sauce would be an added bonus.

2 large ripe bananas or slices from master recipe (see p. 229)

½ cup flour

3 tablespoons sugar

2 eggs

½ cup milk

⅛ teaspoon salt

½ cup vegetable or coconut oil, for frying

Chocolate Sauce

1 cup chocolate pieces

⅔ cup whipping cream

1 teaspoon strong coffee

A pinch of sea salt

▶ Slice bananas into 2.5 cm (1 in) pieces.

▶ Mix the flour and sugar together in a medium-sized bowl.

▶ In another smaller bowl, beat the eggs, milk and salt together.

▶ Whisk the milk mixture into the flour mixture. Set aside for 10 minutes.

▶ Warm the oil in a small saucepan. Dip the banana slices into the batter and then place directly into the oil. The bananas are cooked when the batter turns golden brown.

▶ Remove from the oil and drain on paper towels. Serve immediately with ice cream and chocolate sauce.

Chocolate sauce

▶ Slowly melt chocolate, cream and coffee together in a small saucepan.

▶ When the mixture is fully melted and smooth, add a pinch of salt and serve.

Banana cream pies with peanut brittle

MAKES 6 MINI PIES OR ONE LONG RECTANGULAR ONE

My husband loves any type of banana cream pie so I decided to create one just for him. My favourite part of this recipe is how light it is with its delicious banana flavour and peanut crunch on top.

Pastry

1 sheet of store-bought puff pastry, thawed

3 bananas, sliced diagonally

Pastry cream

1 cup milk

¼ cup half-and-half or heavy cream

1 vanilla bean, split down the middle and seeds scraped out

4 large egg yolks, lightly beaten

⅓ cup sugar

3 tablespoons cornflour

1 tablespoon butter

1 ripe banana, mashed

Do not throw away the egg whites. Place them in a small container and freeze for later use for an egg white omelet or meringues.

Rinse the vanilla pod and drop it into a bottle of vodka to infuse for a few weeks.

Pastry

▶ Preheat the oven to 200°C (400°F).

▶ Roll out the puff pasty into one large rectangle.

▶ Place individual pie plates over the pastry and cut around the forms, allowing enough dough to cover the base and sides of the plates.

▶ Carefully lift the pastry and place into the pie plates. Use your fingers to mould to shape, allowing the pastry to overhang a little (the pastry shrinks during baking). Prick the base of the pastry using a fork.

▶ Bake for 10–15 minutes, or until nicely puffed and light golden brown in colour. Allow the pastry shells to cool.

Pastry cream

▶ In a medium saucepan, bring ½ cup of the milk, the fresh cream and the vanilla bean to a simmer, then switch off the heat and allow the flavours to steep.

▶ In a separate bowl, whisk together the egg yolks and sugar until the granules begin to dissolve. Whisk in the rest of the milk and the cornflour. Set aside.

▶ Remove the vanilla bean from the cream mixture. Pour the warm cream mixture over the egg mixture, then pour the combination back into the saucepan.

▶ Heat the mixture over medium heat. Do not have the heat too high otherwise the eggs will scramble.

▶ Once the mixture thickens – it could take 5–10 minutes – remove from the heat and stir in the butter until fully melted.

▶ Place the base of the saucepan in a waiting ice bath and continue stirring until the mixture cools and has a smooth consistency.

▶ Place plastic wrap directly onto the surface of the mixture and place the saucepan in the fridge until cooled fully.

▶ Remove bowl from fridge, mix in mashed banana. Whip the ½ cup of whipping cream until peaks form then fold in ¼ of cream at a time. Return to refrigerator until ready to use.

Peanut brittle

1 cup sugar

¼ cup water

½ tablespoon butter

1 teaspoon vanilla essence

½ cup peanuts, lightly chopped

Peanut brittle

▶ Line a baking sheet with parchment paper or a silicone mat.

▶ In a heavy saucepan, over low heat, melt the sugar and water together. Increase the heat and bring the mixture to a boil. Allow to boil, swirling occasionally, until a deep amber colour is achieved.,

▶ Mix in the butter, vanilla and peanuts.

▶ Immediately pour the mixture onto the baking sheet and allow to cool.

To serve

▶ Placed the sliced bananas over the base of pastry shells. Spoon the cream filling over the bananas.

▶ Break up the peanut brittle and sprinkle decoratively over the cream.

Need a chocolate fix? Sprinkle chocolate chips over the hot brittle mixture once it has been poured over the peanuts and use a small spatula to spread the chocolate. Allow to cool then break into pieces.

Pear

I have always loved pears, fresh or poached. My favourite dessert growing up was poire belle Hélène (pears poached in sugar syrup with chocolate sauce and ice cream). I remember staying at the Hyde Park Hotel with my family and sneaking into the ornate dining room with my grandfather to share one of these delicious desserts. We loved being accomplices when it came to sneaking sweets, which were a rarity in my family.

Master recipe

Poached pears

SERVES 6

6 large pears (Bartlett and
Comice are too soft)

2 litres (2 quarts) water

2 cups sugar

1 vanilla bean

▸ Peel the pears, leaving a small
circle of skin around the stem.
If you decide to cut the pears in
half, all the skin can be removed.

▸ To keep the pears from
discoloring while you make the
syrup, place in a bowl of water
with a little lemon juice.

▸ Place the 2 litres of water and
the sugar in a large saucepan and
bring to a boil for 2–3 minutes.
Reduce the heat and place the
peeled pears in the liquid.

▸ Split the vanilla bean in half, scrap
out the seeds, and then put the
seeds and pod in the liquid with
the pears.

▸ Cover the pears with a circle of
parchment paper and cook for
10–20 minutes (the time depends
on the size and type of pear). The
pears are ready when a paring
knife can slip through the flesh
without any resistance. Be careful
not to overcook the pears. It is
better to keep them a bit hard
rather than overcooked and
mushy.

▸ Remove the pears and vanilla bean, turn up the heat and reduce the
poaching liquid to half, at least 20 minutes or more. Allow to cool.

▸ Pour the reduced cooled syrup over the pears and store in the fridge for
up to 5 days.

HEALTH BENEFITS

The high level of pectin (fibre) in pears is beneficial for regulating cholesterol levels as well as healthy bowels.

Pears have a high level of vitamin C, which helps to boost the immune system.

The high level of anti-oxidants and carotenoids in pears are effective in reducing the risk of age-related macular degeneration.

Drinking a glass of pear juice has a cooling effect and is excellent in relieving fever or heat-related symptoms on a hot day.

Pears have a low GI rating, which is essential in the management of diabetes and the prevention of heart-related disease.

BUYING AND STORING GUIDE

When buying pears, look for firm, bruise-free fruit. To ensure ripeness, press lightly around the stem, if there is some give, the pear is ready to be eaten.

Since pears ripen from the inside out, if the outer layer is soft, there is no doubt that the pear will be close to rotting on the inside.

Place pears in a paper bag, at room temperature, to speed up the ripening process. Once ripe, place them in the fridge but keep them away from smelly food since pears absorb odours.

Pears are delicate fruit to ship so they are often picked and received in stores unripe. They become sweet and juicy over time while they ripen on your counter and stay ripe for a few days in the fridge.

Pear skin becomes tough when cooked so it is best to peel them before cooking. The white flesh turns brown once the skin is removed so it is best to leave them to soak in a lemon juice and water bath until ready to use.

Poaching or cooking pears is the best way to store them for any extended period of time.

GREEN FINGERS

Pears are members of the rose family, and are also closely related to apples and quinces.

If going to a u-pick farm, look for healthy pears that have fallen from the tree. That is a sign that pears are ready to be harvested.

Pears can be grown in bottles, as they do in Europe. After the tree has flowered, a bottle is placed over the budding fruit. Once a pear has grown to maturity, the bottle and fruit is plucked from the tree. A spirit of choice is then added to the bottle and the pear is allowed to ferment for 6 months. This is a rewarding yet labour-intensive project to undertake if you happen to have a pear tree in your garden.

It is best to eat a raw pear with the skin intact since that is where most of the fibre is stored but poaching pears is a good alternative to throwing them out.

The stem and core can be fed to the compost heap or worms.

5 cups bread pieces, torn up using stale bread

2 cups cubed poached pears (master recipe, see p. 237)

¼ cup flaked toasted almonds

3 eggs

½ cup brown sugar

1 cup whipping cream

1 cup milk

1 teaspoon ground cinnamon

½ teaspoon freshly grated nutmeg

1 teaspoon amaretto liqueur or vanilla essence

Store almonds in freezer to reduce the risk of them turning rancid.

Topping

¼ cup ground almonds

¼ cup brown sugar

Toast almonds by heating up a dry frying pan and letting them brown. The oil in the almonds is enough lubricant for the pan.

Almond and pear bread pudding with a caramelized topping

SERVES 6

This is a great recipe to use up leftover bread. I like to use egg or challah bread because of its consistency. Croissants are also a good choice.

▸ Grease 6 large ramekins with butter (or one 2-litre [2-quart] ovenproof dish).

▸ Toss the bread, pears and almonds together in a bowl and use the mixture to fill the prepared ramekins to the top.

▸ Whisk the eggs and sugar together in a medium bowl.

▸ Whisk the cream, milk, cinnamon, nutmeg and amaretto (or vanilla) into the egg and sugar mixture.

▸ Pour the batter evenly over the pear mixture in the ramekins. Press down with the back of a spoon to ensure that all the cubes are well soaked with the mixture. Set aside for 1 hour or cover in the fridge overnight.

▸ Preheat the oven to 180°C (350°F).

▸ Just before baking, mix the sugar and ground almonds together and sprinkle over the top of the bread pudding. Bake for about 45 minutes until the custard is set. Less time (25 minutes) is needed if cooking in ramekins.

▸ Let the bread pudding stand for about 20 minutes before unmoulding or serving with vanilla ice cream.

This dessert can also be made with overripe raw pears, just bake for a little longer.

Poire belle Hélène

SERVES 6

This is my favorite food memory of all the recipes in this book. There are so many ways to present this dessert of poached pears, ice cream and chocolate sauce that it is up to you to be creative.

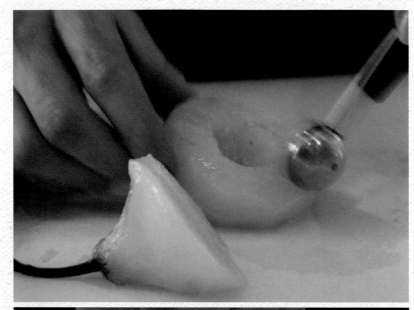

6 poached pears (master recipe, see p. 237)

¼ cup pear poaching liquid

½ cup heavy cream

½ cup dark chocolate chunks

2 pinches of sea salt

Vanilla ice cream

2 tablespoons chopped toasted pistachios

▶ Bring ¼ cup of poaching liquid and the cream to a boil in a small saucepan.

▶ Remove from the heat and mix the chocolate chunks into the hot liquid. Stir until a smooth sauce is achieved. Add 2 pinches of sea salt.

▶ Place a pear half in a glass bowl. Add a scoop of vanilla ice cream. Pour warm chocolate sauce over the ice cream and sprinkle with chopped pistachios.

If no poaching liquid is available, use simple syrup (see p. 69)

let's make better mistakes tomorrow...

Pear, Gorgonzola and steak salad

SERVES 6

This is a great salad to use up leftover steak or a great Sunday salad to serve to guests with a loaf of crusty bread and a glass of red wine.

2 tablespoons grated ginger

4 cloves garlic, minced

½ cup soy sauce

¼ cup maple syrup

2 flank steaks or hanger (skirt) steak

3 poached pears (master recipe, see p. 237) or fully ripened

4 cups mixed lettuce leaves, including rocket and baby greens

1 wedge Gorgonzola or other blue cheese, crumbled

2 tablespoons apple cider vinegar

1 tablespoon Dijon mustard

1 teaspoon maple syrup

2 tablespoons poaching liquid reserve from poaching pears

¼ cup olive oil

1 tablespoon chopped fresh flat-leaf parsley

Salt and pepper to taste

¼ cup spicy maple nuts (see below)

Spicy maple nuts

2 tablespoons brown sugar

1 tablespoon butter

1 tablespoon maple syrup

½ cup pecan nuts

¼ teaspoon chilli powder

▶ In a shallow, flat dish, mix together the ginger, garlic, soy sauce and maple syrup. Marinate the steaks in this mixture overnight.

▶ Heat the grill and cook the steaks to desired doneness. Medium-rare is best for a flank steak. Set aside for 10 minutes before carving. When cutting the steak, be sure to cut against the grain.

▶ While the steak is cooking, cut the poached pears into slivers.

▶ Place the mixed lettuce leaves in a large bowl. Add the pears and crumbled gorgonzola.

▶ In a small bowl, whisk together the apple cider vinegar and Dijon mustard. When thickened, add a few drops of maple syrup and poaching liquid. Put a towel under the bowl, to secure it, and start slowly pouring oil into the vinegar mixture while constantly mixing to create an emulsion. Add parsley at the end as well as salt and pepper.

▶ Once the dressing is ready, toss a little into the salad and arrange the steak pieces on top. Sprinkling with nuts and serve immediately.

Spicy maple nuts

▶ Line a baking sheet with a silicone mat or parchment paper.

▶ Stir the sugar, butter and maple syrup together in a small saucepan and bring to a simmer.

▶ Add the pecans and stir until well coated. Sprinkle with chilli powder and continue stirring for an additional few minutes.

▶ Pour the mixture onto the prepared baking sheet and allow to cool.

These nuts are also good on the flatbread pizza with prosciutto and pear (see p. 244).

Pear, brie and prosciutto flatbread pizza

SERVES 4–6 AS AN APPETIZER

So simple to make yet so impressive to serve. I like to serve this pizza on a long wooden board with pieces pre-cut to make life easier for everyone. It is up to you to decide on the shape of the pizza.

Flatbread

Flatbread

1¾ cups flour

1 teaspoon baking powder

¾ teaspoon salt

½ cup water

⅓ cup olive oil, plus more for brushing

Sea salt

Flatbread

▸ Preheat the oven to 200°C (400°F).

▸ Sift the flour, baking powder and salt together in a medium bowl. Make a well in the centre, then add the water and oil and gradually stir into flour with one hand until a dough forms.

▸ Knead the dough for a few minutes, then divide in half.

▸ Roll out each ball, one piece at a time (keeping the remaining piece covered with plastic wrap).

▸ Place a round or oblong piece of dough (shape is your choice) on a piece of parchment paper or a silicone mat. Lightly brush the top with additional oil. Sprinkle with sea salt.

▸ Bake until pale golden and browned in spots, 8–10 minutes.

Topping

Topping

1 poached pear (master recipe, see p. 237) or raw

8 slices Brie

8 slices prosciutto

A handful of rocket

Topping

▸ Remove the flatbread from the oven and decorate with pear and Brie slices. Return to the oven briefly to melt the cheese. Once melted, add slices of prosciutto and the rocket leaves. Cut and serve.

When working flour with your hands, always keep one hand clean for unforeseen emergencies.

Homeward bound after Sundowners near Little Kulala, Sossusvlei, Namibia

Index

BY COURSE/DISH

Index